inspired
INTERIORS

GreyHunt Interiors, Chantilly, VA, page 387

Amazing Rooms Imagined and Decorated by the Nation's Leading Interior Designers

Published by
Intermedia Publishing Services, Inc.
5815 Richwater Drive
Dallas, TX 75252
972-898-8915

Publisher: Brian G. Carabet
Regional Publisher: Rick Esposito
Regional Publisher: Marc Zurba
Managing Editor: Lindsey Wilson
Editor: Katrina Autem
Art Director: Adam Carabet
Research Coordinator: Lilla Ivonne Esposito
Production Coordinator: Vicki Lindsey

Copyright © 2021 by Intermedia Publishing Services, Inc.
All rights reserved.

No part of this book may be reproduced or transmitted in any form or by any means, electronic or mechanical, including photocopying, recording, or by any information storage or retrieval system, except brief excerpts for the purpose of review, without written permission of the publisher.

All images in this book have been reproduced with the knowledge and prior consent of the professionals featured herein and no responsibility is accepted by the producer, publisher, or printer for any infringement of copyright or otherwise arising from the contents of this publication. Every effort has been made to ensure that credits accurately comply with the information supplied.

Printed in Malaysia

Distributed by Independent Publishers Group
800.888.4741

PUBLISHER'S DATA

INSPIRED INTERIORS
Amazing Rooms Imagined and Designed by the Nation's Leading Interior Designers

Library of Congress Control Number

ISBN 13: 978-0-578-59137-7

First Printing 2021

10 9 8 7 6 5 4 3 2 1

This publication is intended to showcase the work of extremely talented people. The publisher does not require, warrant, endorse, or verify any professional accreditations, educational backgrounds, or professional affiliations of the individuals or firms included herein. All copy and photography published herein has been reviewed and approved by the featured professionals as free of any usage fees or rights and accurate by the individuals and/or firms included herein.

Intermedia Publishing, is dedicated to the restoration and conservation of the environment. Our books are manufactured with strict adherence to an environmental management system in accordance with ISO 14001 standards, including the use of paper from mills certified to derive their products from well-managed forests. We are committed to continued investigation of alternative paper products and environmentally responsible manufacturing processes to ensure the preservation of our fragile planet.

Celaya / Soloway Interiors, Tucson, AZ, page 384

Ca'Shae Interior Design, Roswell, GA, page 83

Introduction

Interior design has the unique ability to change day-to-day life in unexpected ways. It's an artform that takes the functional rooms of a home, considers all the tasks performed within, and reimagines them through an artist's perspective—all while adding functionality. *Inspired Interiors* is a thoughtfully curated collection of spaces that have been beautifully planned by interior designers and their networks of artisans, fabricators, and skilled contractors.

If you're searching for new ways to freshen up your home, look no further than the image-laden pages of this book. The first of its kind in our approximately 200-book portfolio, *Inspired Interiors* has been segmented with the intention of sparking creativity in your own spaces. Through redesigns, remodels, and new builds, you'll pull ideas, styles, and concepts to implement in your own home or office. Or perhaps the book will inspire you in a smaller way, such as choosing new art for a bold change or redecorating a guest room. Broken into eight chapters, the book explores living rooms, kitchens, bedrooms, bathrooms, dining rooms, outdoor living spaces, specialty spaces, and custom furniture. Within each of those divisions you'll find an array of styles, materials, colors, and textures that are as diverse as the designers and homeowners themselves.

Delve into the kitchens of Laurie McRae and find ways that you too might collaborate with an architect to bring your vision to life. Laurie created a contemporary dream kitchen with walnut panels that hide the rooms typical realities and show off clean, uncluttered lines. Glance into Glenna Stone's New England kitchens for images of timeless, classic beauty. See how her use of light-colored palettes, natural materials, and modern functionality make the kitchen look as important as it actually is to a home. Marvel at the bathroom innovations of Arizona-based Lori Carroll, who turned a plumbing-free, mountainside wine room into a stunning modern bathroom. Or peek into Tanga Winstead's character-filled New Orleans bathroom, set in a classic Uptown shotgun home and featuring a charming clawfoot bathtub and a refurbished medical cabinet that now serves as a linen closet. Find ideas for your backyard or patio with Design Lines' Judy Pickett and her peaceful outdoor respites in the South. Or look to Ginger Atherton, who designs Hollywood-worthy al fresco settings, each full of West Coast glamour and whimsy.

Although the interior designers featured within represent a range of backgrounds, experiences, styles, and approaches, they all possess creativity and an overarching desire to please. But one common trait is critical to the success of every project: heightened listening skills. Each designer has taken the unique components of a space, the wishes of the homeowners, and a set of issues that will undoubtedly arise while working, and made it all come together beautifully. Without the ability to hone in and really hear what the clients are requesting, reading between the lines, and understanding the details of a lifestyle, none of these visions would have come to life. It's no wonder that in the process of designing interiors, so many friendships are forged.

Sit back with a fresh cup of coffee, or snuggle up with a nice glass of wine, and absorb the masterful work of some of the country's most talented interior designers showcased in over 800 thought-provoking photographs in the following pages of *Inspired Interiors*.

Enjoy,

Brian G. Carabet
Publisher

Shane Spencer, Minneapolis, MN, page 391

ML Interiors, Dallas, TX, page 389

8 INSPIRED INTERIORS

"My approach is to create harmony and a sense of simplicity, yet never be ordinary. Through the use of color, textures, and fascinating materials, my designs seek to provide engaging environments that delight the senses."
— Esther Boivin, Esther Boivin Interiors

Kamarron Design, Inc, Minneapolis, MN, page 455

"My interest is in finding a cooperative balance between funky and sophisticated. So the true test of a finished, successful project is how it enhances the unique lives of my client."
—Kara A. Bigos, Kamarron Design, Inc

Legacy Interiors, N. Myrtle Beach, SC, page 388

Carson Guest, Atlanta, GA page 384

Pamela Hope Designs, Houston, TX, page 890

"Inspiration is everywhere. While nature provides inspiration for our palettes, architecture does so for detail. However, it is our clients that truly inspire us - we design for them. It's their style preference, preferred palette, and most importantly their lifestyle that dictate our design direction."

—Diane Durocher, Diane Durocher Interiors

Rill Architects, Bethesda, MD, page 390

contents

Living Spaces   21
Unique Living Room, Great Room, Family Room & Sunroom designs to inspire from cozy comfort to dynamic entertaining.

Kitchen Spaces   109
Welcome to the heart of the home, where meals and bonds are forged against backdrops that range from sleek and chic to rustic traditional.

Dining Spaces   179
From formal holidays to everyday meals, break bread in these sophisticated, stylish spaces that encourage you to pull up a chair and stay a while.

Bedroom Spaces   217
The most intimate rooms in a home, these personal retreats are a wealth of sumptuous, escape-worthy ideas.

Bathroom Spaces   263
Whether compact powder rooms or palatial personal saunas, these spa-like spaces encompass everything from serene to high style.

Outdoor Living Spaces   307
Unique outdoor living areas that encourage us to enjoy our cooking, entertaining, and recreational activities from the inside to the outdoors.

Specialty Spaces   331
These home offices, libraries, bars, winerooms, home theaters, exercise rooms, laundry rooms and more will inspire unique rooms.

Custom Furniture   371
Any piece of furniture or built-in that can imagined, can be created, by these talented interior designers with a myriad of finishes and fabrics.

Meet the Designers   382
Learn more about the creative geniuses that imagined, designed and decorated the amazing rooms featured in Inspired Interiors.

Knight Carr & Company, Greensboro, NC, page 388

Living Spaces

Living spaces are chameleons of sorts—they adapt and conform to a variety of needs. They are the rooms for intimate conversation, the venues for parties and gatherings, and the personal family spaces for a wide range of activities. Because of this, they are important areas of a home that require thoughtful design.

Kitchens, bathrooms, bedrooms, offices, dining rooms, and specialty spaces such as theaters or home gyms have specific purposes. They are designed and appointed with appliances, hardware, lighting, storage, and furnishings that establish and enhance their singular function. But living spaces do it all, and can therefore be a challenge to design. They must provide flexibility by creating enough comfort to curl up with a book during a Saturday afternoon, yet give off the energetic vibes for a cocktail party that same evening—this dynamic is what I love about designing them.

To make a living space successful, I focus on three key elements: comfort, lighting, and furniture placement. Comfort is different for every person, and this aspect can be specific to the homeowner or rely on logical details such as including a firm armchair for an elderly family member. A room can be beautiful, but if it's not comfortable, what's the point? Next, lighting should be considered for the flexibility of the space. If a television is present, for example, does the natural light need alteration? And lastly, furniture placement, particularly seating, should be designed for ease of conversation and line-of-sight to individuals, or television viewing, if desired. If the space will serve as an entertainment spot or a holiday gathering room, some of the furnishings may need to be movable to accommodate.

Keep flexibility, comfort, space arrangement, and, of course, beauty in mind if you're looking to create your own living spaces. And don't forget to take advantage of the opportunity for self-expression that interior design allows. Always have fun with it.

Linda Knight Carr
Knight Carr & Company
Greensboro, NC
see page 388

KP Designs, page 388

Design Milieu, page 385

Shannon Antipov, page 391

ABOVE: This casual family room is visible as you step into the gracious entry hall of a Georgian-style home. We set out to create a comfortable gathering place that is also worthy of a first view. For the fabrics, we selected natural fibers with heavy-use potential that also exhibited elegance.

FACING PAGE: We chose a color palette representing the sea, sand, and sunset for a coastal home. The intention was to establish a space for easy living that would always have a mood deserving of the impressive view. This space is central to the dining area and another seating area where a television is prominent. Because of this, the small chairs are meant to move elsewhere as needed, and the club chairs swivel for flexibility.

PREVIOUS PAGE: In this intimate, classically appointed living room, I established a monochromatic color scheme to enhance the sense of spaciousness. Punctuation of color—such as flowers—can be introduced throughout the year with any hue imaginable. The calmness of the space creates an environment for the clients' quiet moments, as well as for entertaining.
Photographs by Dustin Peck
Interiors by Knight Carr & Company, Greensboro, NC, page 388

"Although beauty is in the eye of the beholder, there are some things that seem universally beautiful. Nature in all forms is one of those things."
—Linda Knight Carr

> *"Beautiful and functional spaces should always reflect the inhabitant's personality in an elegant and comfortable way."*
> — Elissa Grayer

ABOVE & FACING PAGE BOTTOM: The client requested that the home be inviting and family-friendly, yet elegant and serene, all against the backdrop of one of Westchester's grandest estates.
Photographs by John Bessler

FACING PAGE TOP: A high-gloss ceiling emphasizes the gorgeous natural light that flows into this apartment, flooding the unique artwork with shimmery light.
Photograph by Regan Wood
Interiors by Elissa Grayer Interior Design, Rye, NY, page 386

BELOW: A luxury residence overlooking the historic Foshay Tower in Minneapolis was completely renovated to create a large entertainment space for gatherings. The client desired relaxed living and a look inspired by the Tuscany countryside. The color palette, comprised of earthtones and luxury textures such as mohair and wool plaid, complemented the design. The center of the space is anchored by a grand limestone fireplace framed by beautifully toned custom bookshelves. Floor-to-ceiling draperies accentuate the spectacular view.
Photographs by Mike McCaw, Spacecrafting
Interiors by Kamarron Design, Inc, Minneapolis, MN, page 387

ABOVE TOP: This long space, with three entries and three focal points, was difficult to design. Cohesion was achieved by floating a custom mohair sectional with a vertically channeled back to enhance the focal points of the lake, limestone-carved fireplace, and entertainment center. Beautifully wrapped in architecture, the original wood was restored and given new luster in this lakeside mansion. The walls, freshly wrapped in wool plaid and a ceiling adorned in a raw silk nub wallpaper, are both from Phillip Jeffries. The hand-woven wool and silk rug pulls you through the space, while anchoring the sectional.

ABOVE BOTTOM: This once-heavy space was swathed in deer antlers and rarely used; now it's a coveted spot to unwind. This space was originally denoted as a screened-in dining space with a barbecue, and was completely transformed. After some structural changes, the walls were clad in a handsome natural stone. This cozy space is located off the pool so the sectional was covered in a durable outdoor Schumacher mohair-like fabric. Art printed on acrylic harkens to the lakeside setting. This beautiful blend of textures, greenery, neutrals, and accessories create a dramatic warmth, making it feel like a space that has been beloved forever. This room was honored with the top National Award Design by IDS.
Photographs by Bill Diers
Interiors by Kamarron Design, Inc, Minneapolis, MN, page 387

RIGHT AND BELOW: Nearly every aspect of this elegant, transitional gathering space is customized. The large window, which sits across from a Brazilian-blue stone fireplace, features push-button Roman shades that allow for sunlight control. Custom bookshelves, outfitted with hand-made iron grills from my shop, show off the client's personal mementos. You'll also find sconces that I made to complement the design of the room.

FACING PAGE: The formal dining room is the center of the home, and in this case, I made it work as both a formal gathering space and a comfortable spot for the family. I incorporated a set of Neoclassical chairs that belonged to the homeowner's mother, which beautifully blended with the Hollywood Regency interior.
Photographs courtesy of Ginger Atherton & Associates
Interiors by Ginger Atherton & Associates, Beverly Hills, CA, page 386

BELOW: Stone and metal make this room both contemporary and warm. Because of the double-height ceiling, the room easily could have felt cold. We focused on creating a connection within the living space and drawing people in, so they would feel comfortable and relaxed.
Photograph by Jon Mancuso

FACING PAGE ABOVE: A benefit to working with metal is it's malleable and can be used at a curved setting. We found creative ways to display the homeowner's art, television, and dramatic fireplace, and ended up with a beautiful, rustic art piece for the living room.
Photograph by Bill Lesch

FACING PAGE BELOW: We are up to any design challenge. The homeowners wanted to use this fireplace and it was a struggle to incorporate metal and tile together in the setting, but we made it work beautifully. The result was an edgy, distinct aesthetic.
Photograph by Bill Lesch

Interiors by Lori Carroll & Associates, Tucson, AZ, page 389

ABOVE: When we reimagined and designed the interiors for a textured Tuscan-style home, we wanted to make a big impact in the formal sitting room since it's the first room you see upon entering. We lightened the house by smoothing the walls' surfaces and using bright colors: white, gold, and ivory. Because the homeowner is from West Texas, the cowhide rug was a fitting choice to soften the space, along with the brilliant blue ottoman and delicate window treatments. Now, Tuscany is a vacation destination instead of a dated home design.
Photograph by Michael Hunter Photography
Interiors by ML Interiors Group, Dallas, TX , page 389

BELOW TOP: Reidentified as a sitting area, this room was originally a formal dining room. We opened it up and used sconces for additional lighting so it can be used for reading and relaxing. And because it's just off the kitchen, the space is also ideal for sharing coffee or enjoying pre-dinner cocktails.

BELOW BOTTOM: Our goal for this family room was to create balance and livability with a Coastal California-meets-Texas-hospitality vibe. We achieved harmony by selecting furniture that works well with the room's large light fixture. As the main gathering spot for a close-knit family of four, this space had to feature performance fabrics. Wine spills, food drops, muddy dog paws, and heavy traffic are fine here, as we opted for stain-resistant, organic materials.
Photographs by Matti Gresham Photography
Interiors by ML Interiors Group, Dallas, TX , page 389

BELOW & FACING PAGE: When we designed the modern Mira Vista home, we aimed to convey a versatile style that intricately flows throughout the floorplan to represent chic beauty. The main living areas feature cool and comfortable greys as well as a rich gold that promote conversation and positivity.
Photographs by Realty Pro Shots
Interiors by Susan Semmelmann Interiors, Fort Worth, TX, page 392

"I aim for personalized spaces that are beautiful and functional, with a traditional soul and modern spirit."
—Lori Graham

ABOVE: The stunning Harlow chandelier by NYC-based design house Gabriel Scott provides both contrast in shape and finish and complement in hue and material to the striking vintage wingbacks.
Photograph by Erik Johnson
Interiors by Lori Graham Design + HOME, Washington, DC, page 389

BELOW TOP: In this living room, we wanted to do something a little different than a standard approach of flanking the fireplace with symmetrical bookshelves. Instead we used the elongated right-hand side of the fireplace for bookshelves and then we installed a large wall mirror on the left-hand side. The wall mirror not only reflects the natural light coming in from the front windows, but it also reflects the art collage on the wall opposite.
Photo by Abby Greenawalt

BELOW BOTTOM LEFT: I love to use a piece of art to inspire a room's décor. The opposite approach, where pieces are selected to match the furnishings, is anathema to me. For clients who have not started their personal collections, we help them find works that might speak to them, and in many cases we work with their own photography of meaningful places, events, or people to make something special to anchor the space.
Photograph by Erik Johnson

BELOW BOTTOM RIGHT: In this larger-scale great room, the custom-designed wall paneling became the art we incorporated into the tall space.
Photograph by Erik Johnson

Interiors by Lori Graham Design + HOME, Washington, DC, page 389

ABOVE & LEFT: These empty nesters—and returning North Carolina residents—wanted a fresh take on traditional design. We worked with builder Rufty Homes to create a living room that felt welcoming enough for kids and grandkids, yet sophisticated and impressive to the adult eye. The wall of windows opens to the porch, which is fitted with Phantom Screens for a seamless outdoor/indoor look. For a touch of interest, we added navy grasscloth to the bookcases to highlight the stone on the fireplace.

FACING PAGE With three young children, the parents at this home were craving an elegant space that felt reserved for them. Family-friendly materials were still used, but the overall effect is serene and chic. Loyd Builders helped make the design of the fireplace the feature that it is, with sconces, molding, and mirrors drawing the eye to the interesting cast stone.
Photographs by Dustin Peck Photography
Interiors by Southern Studio, Cary, NC, page 391

"Every part of the design process has meaning and purpose to satisfy a larger goal."
—Elizabeth O'Neal

LEFT: We wanted the homeowners to be able to enjoy the scope of their large living room without sacrificing intimacy. This was achieved through careful attention to scale—the tall lamps and chairs help offset a soaring ceiling—and the use of layered lighting. Wall sconces and crystal lamps illuminate the space in the evening.
Photograph by Lissa Gotwals Photography

BELOW: Navy, bright blue, and grey give this sitting area its charm. We made a conversation spot that is ideal for relaxing with a glass of wine.
Photographs by Dustin Peck Photography

FACING PAGE TOP: Tradition and elegance come together in a room that showcases the homeowner's love of antiquities. The wall sculpture and art pieces stand out against the soothing verdigreen.
Photograph by Jane Beiles Photography

FACING PAGE BOTTOM: Our departure point for a contemporary living room was Jason Craighead's work of art above the sofa. We incorporated natural materials and gold pieces to complement the painting. You'll also notice beautiful art pieces encased on either side of the sitting area. We chose an antique rug with subtle shades of gold and grey-blue so as to not detract from the art.
Photograph by Brie Williams Photography
Interiors by Design Lines Signature, Raliegh, NC, page 385

BELOW & FACING PAGE: The homeowners have quite an impressive art collection, with Chagalls and other acquisitions from their worldwide collection hanging throughout the home, so I took my color cues from this Ecuadorian painting that we floated over the fireplace. It's matted in the same silk as the draperies, and draws in the greens, golds, oranges, and purples from the nearby dining room.
Photographs by Sèlavie Photography
Interiors by Ami Austin Interior Design, Memphis, TN, page 382

LEFT: The lady of the house wanted a morning room just for herself, so we renovated the sun porch, which has three exposures. Her passions include music and reading—you'll notice sheet music on the lampshade and a designated space for her favorite books. She also wanted to make sure her rescue dogs were comfortable, so we chose a sofa that wasn't too tall and had no arm rests to make it easily accessible for them.

ABOVE LEFT: We designed a contemporary living room for a couple of empty nesters to relax. The TV is nearly hidden above the linear fireplace and this room is ideal for enjoying music. You'll see the homeowners' passion for music reflected in the art piece—its shape mimics a music note. Favorite books are also important here and are on display.

ABOVE RIGHT: As you enter the foyer, there is little to stop the eye from following sight lines to the rear of this home. Infused with Japanese design elements, the entryway connects the living areas to the quiet spaces. You'll notice other Asian elements, such as the Chinese carvings on the wall and nature-inspired light fixture, that add to the overall Zen quality of the home.

FACING PAGE TOP: Set in a 1910 Augusta home, the bar space was an important area to this child-free couple who enjoy having friends over. It includes barstools, a pair of comfortable arm chairs for a conversation spot, and a wall bar for the extra guests to belly up to. Semi-sheer shades filter the light and provide privacy from the street.

Photographs by Steve Bracci Photography
Interiors by Laurie McRae Interiors, Augusta, GA, page 388

BELOW: Everything in the Beaufort home was designed to let its natural surroundings shine. Because the home was a new build, we were able to choose elements that wouldn't detract from the views. For the living room, we went with a neutral palette and an understated, elegant look that welcomes the outside in.

FACING PAGE TOP: Located in Newport Beach, California, this oceanfront home was a complete remodel. We went with a less-is-more approach for the bachelor homeowner and used a white leather sectional to achieve the look he wanted. He has an impressive collection of Murano glass pieces, showcased on the custom limestone wall.

FACING PAGE BOTTOM: We took a traditional two-story living room in this Southern home and made it more intimate. You'll see modern touches used in the complete design renovation that keep the space from being dated. Three children live in this house, so it's intended to be an adult area where the parents can entertain, but it's still comfortable and approachable.
Photographs by Robert Clark
Interiors by LGB Interiors, Columbia, SC, page 389

BELOW TOP: Though new construction, the midcentury modern feel relies on warm colors and natural wood to offset colder materials such as the stone fireplace.

BELOW BOTTOM: The draperies and lamps are elongated to accentuate the room's impressive height, while lots of gold accents and a custom rug create texture.
Photographs by Jessie Preza
Interiors by Lisa Gielincki Interior Design, Jacksonville, FL, page 389

ABOVE LEFT: We kept the floors in this remodel and relied on an array of light colors and new furnishing to create a soft palette that's airy and relaxing.

ABOVE TOP RIGHT: We clad the ceiling in hand-painted wood to highlight the room's architecture, and stained the doors and beams dark for further contrast.

ABOVE BOTTOM RIGHT: The reclaimed brick and rustic doors, when paired with this cheerful and colorful palette, is a very pleasing combination.
Photographs by Jessie Preza
Interiors by Lisa Gielincki Interior Design, Jacksonville, FL, page 389

ABOVE: A large stone art piece adds natural beauty to the living and dining spaces. Hand-chiseled to give the work a refined finish, the stone is as beautiful as it is interesting. Customized elements include the sofa and drapes, which were color matched to the deep indigo walls.
Photograph by Matti Gresham

FACING PAGE TOP: Mixed elements and styles create interest, both with interiors and art. The painting is by David Crismon, an artist who reconstructs Dutch Renaissance portraits into modern interpretations. Light fixtures from Arteriors and a custom sofa and chairs blend beautifully for an eclectic look.
Photograph by Miriam Hill

FACING PAGE BOTTOM: For a collaborative design, we pulled in unexpected pieces that layer beautifully. An African sculpture alongside striking Ted Kinkaid photography, Donghia-covered chairs placed with a custom sofa, and a built-in bookcase with a range of items help create a multi-dimensional space.
Photograph by Jill Woodruff
Interiors by Total 360 Interiors, Dallas, TX, page 392

"When done well, blending styles within a room gives you a curated effect. Layered, mixed elements can create an eclectic, one-of-a-kind room."
—Nancy Black

ABOVE, TOP LEFT & RIGHT: This classic Virginia country home has two parlors off the foyer that were perfect to transform into African- and Asian-themed rooms that hold memories for the globe-trotting homeowners. In the African room, we chose rich textures in a smoky grey palette with red accents, eel-skin wall coverings, and an Italian porcelain-tile fireplace wall with a faux leather texture.

ABOVE, BOTTOM LEFT & RIGHT: The Asian room has three walls covered in a teal metallic backed cork, with the far wall accented in reclaimed wood planks. We added a water feature as a serene backdrop to the Buddha statue, and a chaise basks in sunlight for a place to stretch out and meditate. The window treatment is a hand-blocked Chinoiserie linen, and the valance is a pagoda shape.

FACING PAGE: To fabricate the mantel in the sunroom, an antique Asian door and doorway were disassembled and repurposed. Ceramic tile with a corroded green and copper finish complements the weather-worn wood. We chose rustic woven wallpaper to soften the look of the walls. The shaped valances and Roman shade hems were trimmed with strips of embroidered linen, all hand-sewn to perfection.
Photographs by Quentin Penn-Hollar, QPH Photo
Window treatments fabricated by LHS Designs
Interiors by Kathy Corbet Interiors, Richmond, VA, page 387

"*Good interior design will let you realize possibilities that you never imagined and gain results beyond your dreams and expectations.*"
—Kathy Corbet

ABOVE: The Alexander McQueen rug started our inspiration for the entire space. Creating a design that felt both masculine and bright was critical to the homeowners. Texture was incorporated through elements like velvet upholstery and a hammered-metal finish on the lamps to create richness that kept the rug as the focal point. Lastly, we highlighted the homeowners' incredible collection of fine art throughout the interior.

FACING PAGE: A love of travel and globally influenced style informed the design for this Washington Square West living room, with the client's antique Chinese wooden chairs as the inspiration. The neutral color palette creates a sense of quiet and calm, with patterns and artwork that evoke an East Asian aesthetic.
Photographs by Rachel McGinn Photography
Interiors by Glenna Stone Interior Design, Philadelphia, PA, page 386

"Inspiration does not come from out of the blue; it's like a muscle that must be developed and exercised. The more you see, absorb, and process, the more inspiration you find. Once you train yourself to be open to inspiration, it flows from all corners."
—Glenna Stone

BELOW: We designed a second home for a Nashville client, located in Alys Beach, Florida. The all-white aesthetic may seem like it's not intended for kids, but this space was made with high-performance elements for a family of five. Slip-covered furniture includes a chaise-style bench that allows family members to relax and participate in activities in both the kitchen and living room. The walls and ceilings are plastered with a high-sheen gloss that reflects the natural light and makes the space shine. A smooth flow from indoor to out adds to the home's airy appeal.
Photograph by Jack Gardner
Interiors by Brad Ramsey Interiors, Nashville, TN, page 383

> *"The journey from house to home is so much richer when I really get to know my clients."*
> —Brad Ramsey

ABOVE: It made sense for us to showcase international-inspired items for a couple who loves to travel. We chose a tribal look with warm tones and rich textures, then pulled in different patterns. You'll notice an African shell necklace, imported oars, and black shale statues displayed in the room. The coffee table is about 65-by-50 inches and serves as the room's focal point. Thanks to the sunlight that pours through the windows, you can see the table's cracked surface with natural variations; it gives the entire space an organic quality. A trio of chandeliers offers a mobile-like aesthetic and utilizes the room's impressive height.
Photographs by Jack Gardner
Interiors by Brad Ramsey Interiors, Nashville, TN, page 383

LEFT: Clean lines with a soothing palette was the theme for this master sitting room. Our clients did not want to obstruct the view of their property with fussy window treatments and opted for the textural simplicity of the woven shades. Textures played an important part of the design, from the smooth chenille upholstered pieces and faux leather storage ottoman to the lush pile of the trellis-pattern Oushak rug.

FACING PAGE & BELOW: The 22-foot-high ceiling of this great room in our client's Georgian-style home was emphasized by the fireplace and drapery panels that frame the view of their beautiful property. The palette of creamy white with pale blue accents is bright and airy, giving fresh appeal to a traditional design. The grand Sheridan-style bookcase and curved credenza create a strong silhouette against the soft white panel molding. The Chesterfield sofas are traditional in nature while the bench is more contemporary. Balance and contrast, new and old, was an ongoing theme.

BELOW BOTTOM RIGHT: Balance and symmetry were important when designing the living room in this sprawling Manor-style home. We painted the walls a pale sand color, which offers a slight contrast to the trim and is the perfect backdrop for our furniture and America Martin contemporary artwork. The ceiling, which is painted a pale blue, is balanced with the paisley silk and wool rug that anchors the seating area. Pale blue, which is our accent color, is repeated with the drapery panels that frame the windows.

FACING PAGE TOP: The great room's large, open floorplan allows for two separate seating areas, which are articulated by custom area rugs. A marble-topped table and stunning floral arrangement divide these two areas while creating a focal point from the entry hallway. Floor-to-ceiling windows, which soar upward to the 22-foot ceilings, open out onto the home's spectacular views and are emphasized by gold satin panels.
Photographs by Peter Rymwid
Interiors by Diane Durocher Interiors, Ramsey, NJ, page 386

"Of course the wishes of our clients guide our work, but ultimately my inspiration comes from nature and the beauty that only God can create."
—Rita Carson Guest

ABOVE LEFT & RIGHT: The animals in this home are as much a part of the family as any human, so the interior had to work for them too. The homeowners give the animals their own zones, leaving the back deck and backyard accessible through a laundry room doggy door, so the dogs can go in and out throughout the day. The kitties have the master suite as well as their own feeding room. In the afternoons, the kitties enjoy resting on the Kagan chairs in the living room. The first to enjoy the Kagan sofa were the pups. The walls of windows allow the dogs to look out and keep watch over the house and their humans.
Photographs by Aaron Leitz Photography
Architect: Daniel Fletcher / Architects PC
Interiors by Carson Guest, Atlanta, GA, page 384

BELOW: The great room is a flexible area that provides subtle demarcations for a living area, kitchen, dining, bar, and play spaces. It's appropriate for up to 200 guests, yet it features intimate areas that are ideal for smaller gatherings. The space combines traditional function with an innovative, one-of-a kind design.

FACING PAGE TOP: The modern desert home's great room shows off angular lines in the walls and ceiling soffits that continue the overall design philosophy. From dark wood ceilings, sleek white walls, and dark-textured stone on the fireplace, the contrast in tones and textures accentuate the architectural details.

FACING PAGE CENTER: For a home set in a rugged desert environment, we took cues for color and texture from the surrounding native canyon. The soft texture of a pewter limestone wall and neutral-tone horizontal fireplace affords this great room a casual, warm ambience.

FACING PAGE BOTTOM: When we worked on a homesite surrounded by stunning mountains, we wanted to show them off, and used window walls to do so. Central is the iron-peak stacked-stone wall traversing from outside to inside, set as a complement to the white oak floor and contrasting darker ceiling.
Photographs by Kurt Munger
Interiors by Celaya | Soloway Interiors, Tucson, AZ, page 384

FACING PAGE TOP: This contemporary, transitional family living room has a cozy, lived-in look, but it still feels crisp with custom contemporary furniture made of kiln-dried, Alder wood from sustainably harvested forests and hard solid maple wood with premium finishes and upholstery treatments. The stone textured fireplace wall makes a bold and sleek statement.

FACING PAGE BOTTOM: The random-length, prefinished, wire brush white oak engineered flooring creates the hominess in this open-concept family room. A custom-made ivory white display bookcase with an exceptional 3-D wallpaper backing gives the space an elegant overall look.

ABOVE: In favor of clean and straight lines, white, beige, and even some shades of black are the main color palette of this modern two-story residence in Bel Air. The interior incorporates shades of gold as an accent to convey a sense of luxury. Commissioned artwork arrangements, custom furniture, and a one-of-a-kind, award-winning swivel chair enhance the appearance of this beautiful yet comfy living family space.
Photographs courtesy of GAVIN GREENE HOME DESIGN LLC
Interiors by GAVIN GREENE HOME DESIGN LLC, page 386

"Inspiration can always be found in the family that will be living there."
— Aven Kaga

ABOVE TOP: Attached to what was once a bleach factory, this penthouse sits across from the French Quarter with impressive views of the Mississippi River. It was important to the client that nothing block or rise above the windows, which allow for light to pour in and show the character of the architecture. The space includes myriad shapes—notice the cow-hide rugs and geometrical furniture—made warm with a variety of textures: leather, wood, linen, and even faux chinchilla on the modern scoop chair.

ABOVE BOTTOM: Set on historic St. Charles Avenue, the period stone house was converted into condos. This particular space works as a multi-purpose setting: a den, living space, office, and second bedroom. The sofa pulls out into a full-size bed to accommodate overnight guests. Created by local artist Ashley Longshore, the custom painting adds to the room's fun, eclectic vibe.

FACING PAGE: Man caves don't have to be hyper-masculine. For a guest bedroom-turned-living space where the husband watches television and relaxes, I added in a few feminine elements so the wife also feels welcome. The Mitchell Gold + Bob Williams chair and ottoman add a plush, feline touch, while the custom chartreuse pillow from a Magazine Street boutique offers a vibrant pop of color.
Photographs by Kerri McCaffety

Interiors by Tanga Winstead Designs, New Orleans, LA, page 392

BELOW TOP: This fun yet elegant high-rise home reflects the personality of an active young family. The casual wood floor and leather cocktail ottoman contrast with the cream textured sofas. Linen printed drapery and glass beaded silk cornices frame the beautiful views of the Gulf. The square-designed beams on the ceiling add to the drama with can and rope lighting hidden in the crown molding. We created a niche for the TV just above the linear fireplace, which is tiled in pen shell tile.

BELOW BOTTOM & FACING PAGE: A lighter wood floor and white marble water-jet fireplace wall contrast with the dark cabinetry and onyx cocktail table. The octagonal ceiling is covered with tongue-and-groove wood and heavy wood beams, showcasing a statement-making silverleaf chandelier with dangling crystals. We used settees made with custom fabric in the dining room to create a cozy and intimate feel. Laminated beams flow into the kitchen and create a flawless transition. Floating cabinets with custom-made hardware and shelves display beautiful accessories that pull the entire room together.
Photographs by Sam Arnold, HomeAndDesignPhotography.com
Interiors by Aniko Designs, Fort Myers, FL, page 382

ABOVE: With the restoration of a 1920s Tudor-style McBirney mansion in Tulsa, the goal was that the rooms could be timeless enough to exist in their original time period, or today. I chose a neutral color palette so that the far left glass sculpture from Kreg Kallenberger, with whom the homeowners are friends, could stand out. Views of the river are unobstructed by draperies, though light-filtering shades are ready to tame the late-afternoon sun when necessary. All the light fixtures in the home are original, having been restored and rewired, and it's very special to have these original pieces still in service.

FACING PAGE: The fabrics and color choices of this room were guided by the warmth we wanted it to project. There's a lot of seating for family and friends around the games tables, while magiscope side tables by Feliciano Bejar spark conversation—as does the custom hair-on-hide coffee table, the hide of which came from the owners' cattle ranch.
Photographs by Ryan Magnani
Interiors by Chad Renfro Design, Palm Beach, FL, page 384

"Work in contrast wherever possible—it will heighten both elements and draw out their best qualities."
—Chad Renfro

68 INSPIRED INTERIORS

RIGHT: I originally wanted to change the paneling in this show house's library, but now I'm glad I didn't because dark wood is making a comeback. The room is very large but still warm and inviting—perfect for a book club.
Photograph by Angie Seckinger

BELOW BOTTOM RIGHT: Another example of splurging strategically is hanging one mirror on top of another. It creates a sense of openness while providing a little bit of bling.
Photograph by Stacy Zarin Goldberg

BELOW BOTTOM LEFT: Making sure a color scheme flows from room to room is important, especially if you're using memorable colors like apple green, blue, and white. Faux green leather and durable fabrics can hold up to the young family, while the grand piano is more than a decoration—the lady of the house is a professional singer.
Photograph by Angie Seckinger

FACING PAGE TOP: This home is quite grand, with 10-foot ceilings and lots of space to entertain. The hall table can actually expand to seat extra dinner guests, or serve as an extra buffet as everyone arrives.
Photograph by Kip Dawkins

Interiors by Kelley Proxmire, Inc., Bethesda, MD, page 388

BELOW TOP: The design of this living space is based on the concept of a contemporary hotel lounge. The layout creates an atmosphere perfect for entertaining by using separate yet connected seating arrangements. Large-scale artwork and a modern statement chandelier, combined with neutral graphic patterns and rich metallic accents, reinforce the sophisticated ambience.
Photograph by Dean J. Birinyi, Dean J. Birinyi Photography

BELOW BOTTOM: Deep, comfortable seating with ample storage and custom touches creates a family space ideal for watching a movie, reading a book, or just comfortably unwinding. Architectural details, new furnishings and light fixtures, and a revised color scheme help bring this space to life. A custom built-in is added in the niche to house the TV and media equipment, and to provide additional storage.
Photograph by David Duncan Livingston
Interiors by Raashi Design, San Ramon, CA, page 390

ABOVE: Two conversation areas sit back-to-back, separated by a console table, in this relaxed yet luxurious great room. The gold and metallic accents bring energy to the neutral color palette. The black, painted accent wall looks striking against the white mantel and faux fur benches, while the artwork is accentuated with a museum-grade spotlight. The smaller conversation area consists of a pair of grey chairs and a bronze drum table with gold detail, while tone-on-tone silver beaded pillows and a gold leaf-shaped tray add a bit of bling.
Photographs by Dean J. Birinyi, Dean J. Birinyi Photography
Interiors by Raashi Design, San Ramon, CA, page 390

ABOVE: The goal of these combined living areas was to have as few partitions as possible, to open up the spaces so they could communicate with each other while still having a sense of scale, texture, and individuality. The exposed steel beams that replaced walls and decorative screens on the balcony above add character. Mixing materials creates an industrial look, blending the natural elements with more refined lighting and furniture.
Photograph by Stacy Zarin Goldberg
Interiors by Rill Architects, Bethesda, MD, page 390

BELOW TOP: The renovation of a historic steel home with no interior structural walls presents its own challenges. The structure is entirely outside of the house, so it appears as though everything floats. The concrete floor is a stark contrast to the beauty beyond the floor-to-ceiling windows. Light fixtures and furniture are used for a sense of scale and to break down the spaces, while the stone emerges out of the ground.
Photograph by Eric Taylor

BELOW BOTTOM LEFT: The volume and grandeur were there in this historic Georgetown property—the rooms just needed to be polished a bit. Adding color creates interest, while window treatments, lighting, and new furniture soften the space.
Photograph by Kip Dawkins

BELOW BOTTOM RIGHT: The family room on a farmhouse property presents a nod to the outbuilding's barn doors, which become a focal point of the space. The wood also contrasts the formality of the trim, with coffers breaking the scale of the wide expanse of ceiling.
Photograph by Angie Seckinger
Interiors by Rill Architects, Bethesda, MD, page 390

74　INSPIRED INTERIORS

BELOW TOP: The interiors of this concrete block home built in 1940 were reimagined to create a canvas for the owners' immense collection of important art, sculpture, and 20th-entury furniture designs. A view from the media room to the minimalist kitchen provides a glimpse of custom ebonized cabinetry, white quartz counters, and a handmade marble backsplash. The bronze and leather barstools from Kelly Wearstler are inviting and sculptural.

BELOW BOTTOM: A well-loved cloud sofa from Restoration Hardware has prominence of place in this media room and family hangout off the kitchen. A vintage walnut credenza allows the Pierre Chareau small 'nun' table lamp—an antique created in 1924 that the owner brought back from Paris—to shine.

LEFT & FACING PAGE BOTTOM: The expansive lower-level living room looks out onto the ravine below. The rare Gio Ponti cocktail table was found in London, while many of the furnishings were custom-made by local craftsmen and fellow designers in the industry. The palette is neutral to showcase the art, with a pop of color in the plum-colored modern sofa and a pair of club chairs from Kelly Wearstler in a deep textural silk.
Photographs by Dale Clark, Arc Photography
Artwork from Brandt-Roberts Galleries, Ecce Gallery, and Kelly Wearstler Studio
Interiors by Spencer Design Associates, Minneapolis, MN, page 391

LEFT: The client wanted to turn what was originally an awkward TV niche into a focal point for the reading corner, so we designed an asymmetrical, two-sided fireplace framed with quartzite and a wrap-around floating oak mantel.
Photograph by Jen Burner

BELOW RIGHT: This grand living room previously had dark beige paint and old carpet, but painting the walls a bright white bounces light across the room and dark espresso wood floor planks anchor the space.
Photograph by Jen Burner

BELOW & FACING PAGE BOTTOM: This true modern farmhouse demanded cozy touches and a casual aesthetic without having a trendy or cliché farmhouse look. Warm wood tones and leathers wrap the space, creating a cohesive and natural feel, while plush performance upholstery in blues, creams, and greys keep it practical and inviting.
Photograph by Matti Gresham

FACING PAGE TOP LEFT: The massive open floorplan of this new build makes the living room, dining room, and kitchen one long, cathedral-like space. Our challenge was to figure out how to keep the space open while creating uniquely defined areas.
Photograph by Matti Gresham

FACING PAGE TOP RIGHT: This family has two young children and a light, bright, California-cozy style. In order to keep the space as family-friendly as possible without losing the integrity of their aesthetic, every piece we chose could either be wiped down easily (woods, metals, plastics) or had performance-fabric for easy cleaning and durability.
Photograph by Jen Burner
Interiors by Brett Nicole Interiors, The Colony, TX, page 383

ABOVE: A modern farmhouse remodel—emphasis on "modern"— relies on a variety of textures to feel fresh and inviting. Lush cut velvets, reclaimed wood, hair-on-hide, and Mongolian fur are just a few of the materials that come together in a sophisticated, interesting way.

FACING PAGE: This cozy man cave features a subtle nautical theme, with warm woods and mixed metals upping the industrial vibe. The rich upholstery and chic leather invite you to stay a while. Black and white elements, especially the segmented artwork featuring Muhammed Ali, further the masculine ambience.
Photographs by Gethro Genius, Quantized Pixels
Interiors by Sanctuary Rooms, Glenarden, MD, page 390

"Great design has the power to shift atmospheres. It contributes heavily to the well-rounding of human health and wellness."
—Shakirah Fayson

"A livable type of luxury is about creating spaces that support and enhance your wellness and well-being."
—Tanya Shively

LEFT: Built and designed by a local top architect, this home kept its clean, contemporary aesthetic through a new front door and surround of leaded glass design that's reminiscent of the desert. A custom wool rug directs your attention to the seating grouping, which remains light and bright through neutral colors.

BOTTOM: The desert views are complemented by natural materials, especially the redwood ceiling, which makes the vast room feel cozier. Two seating areas—one for conversation by the fireplace and the other for watching TV—are connected through matching sofas, helping the space to appear friendlier and more usable.

FACING PAGE: A request for more color doesn't have to mean bold choices in paint. The great view onto the patio and golf course beyond is highlighted with a warm sand color on the walls, accented by native ledge stone and a copper fireplace surround. Pocket doors that open completely erase the line between indoors and out, making the room ideal for entertaining. Rich wood brings the ceiling down to a more personal level.
Photographs by Jerry Portelli, Architectural Photographic Specialists
Interiors by Sesshu Design Associates, Scottsdale, AZ, page 391

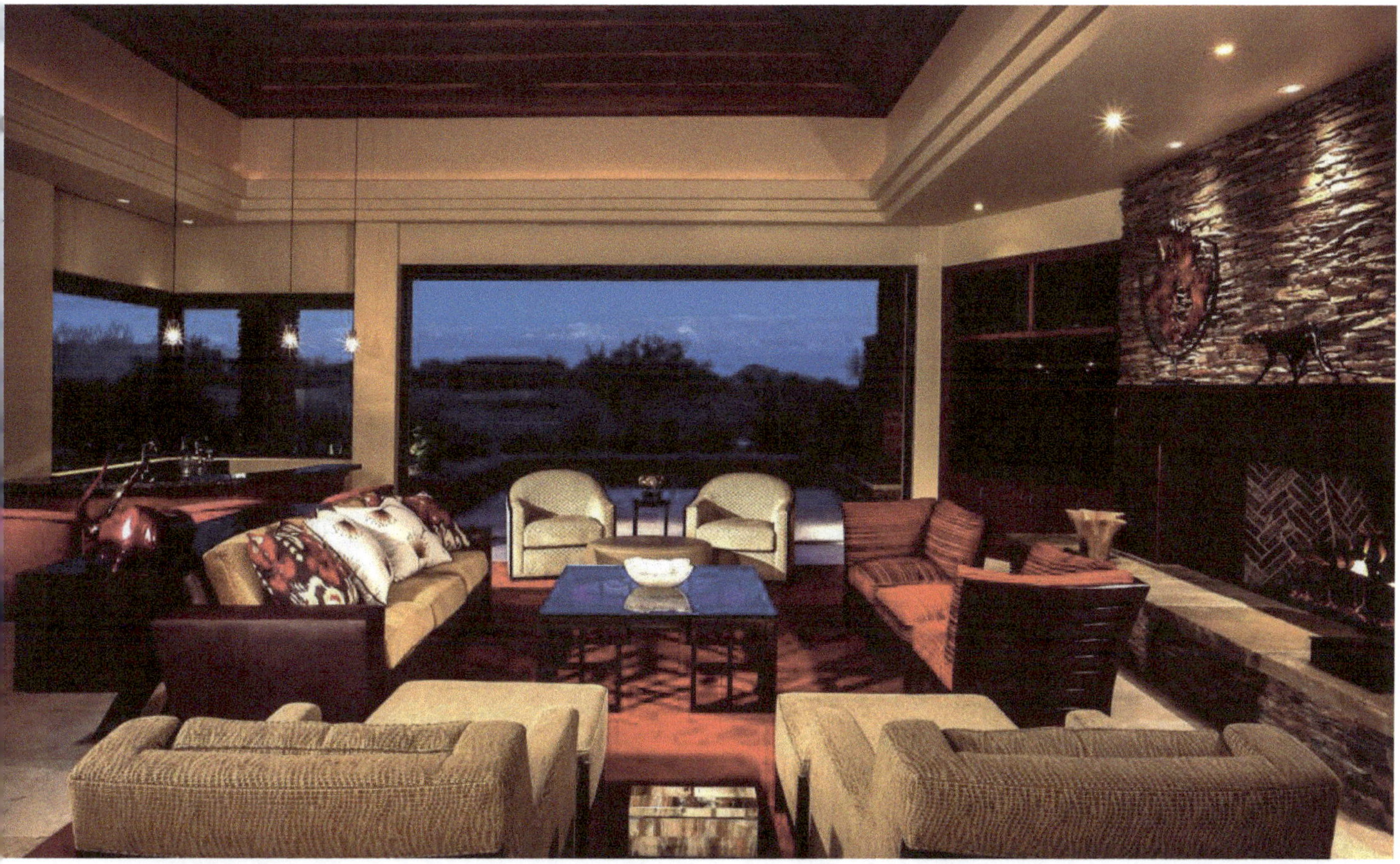

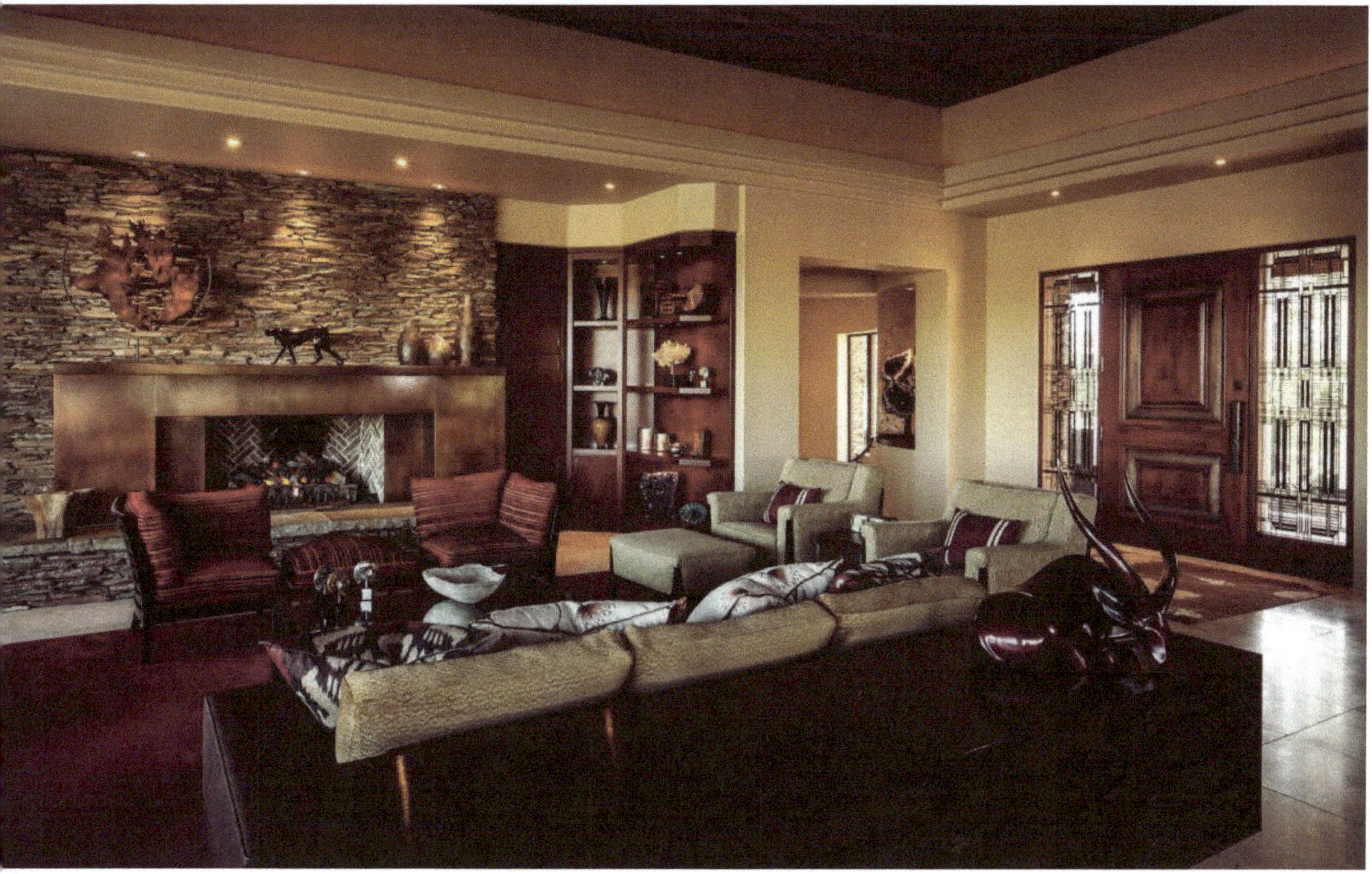

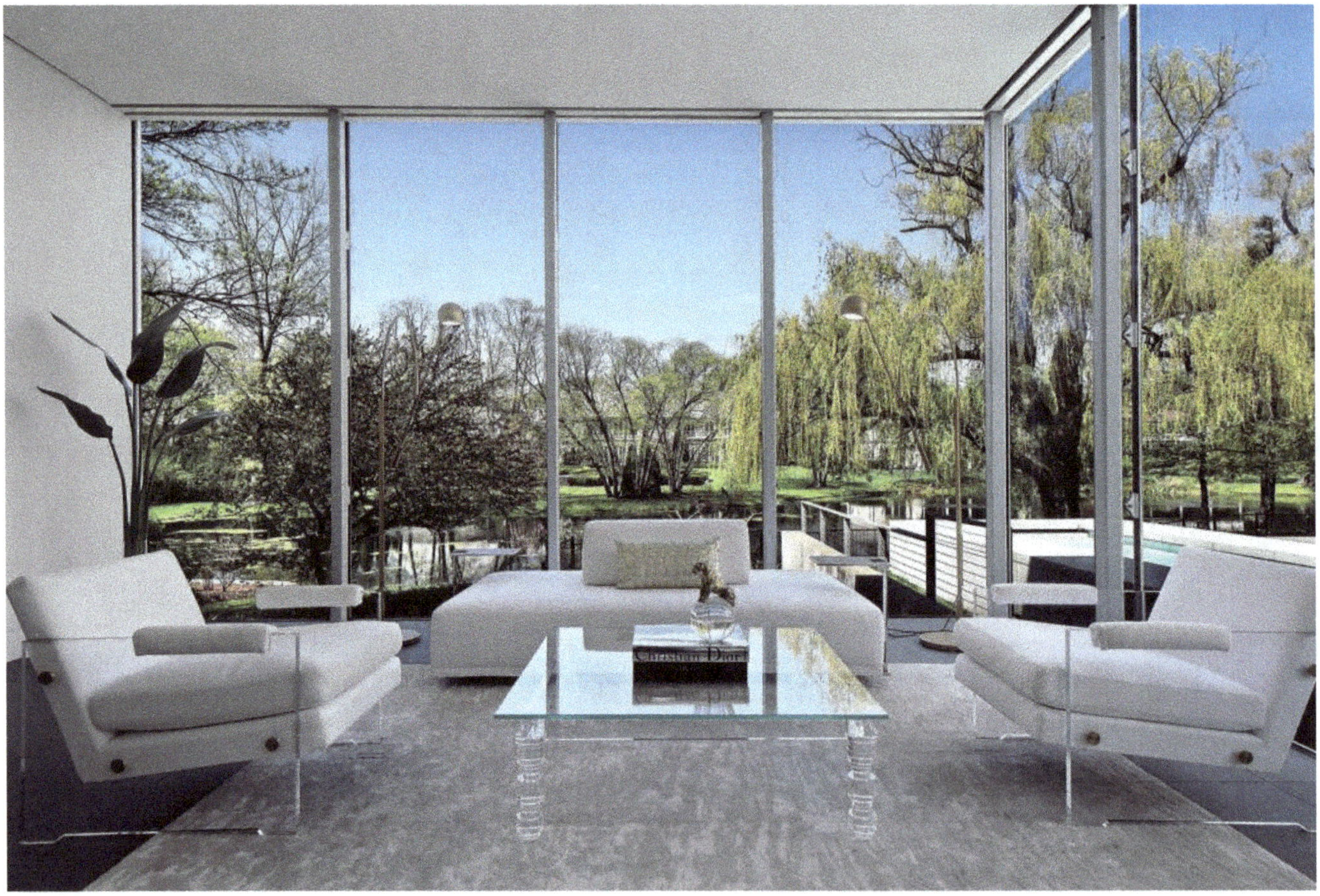

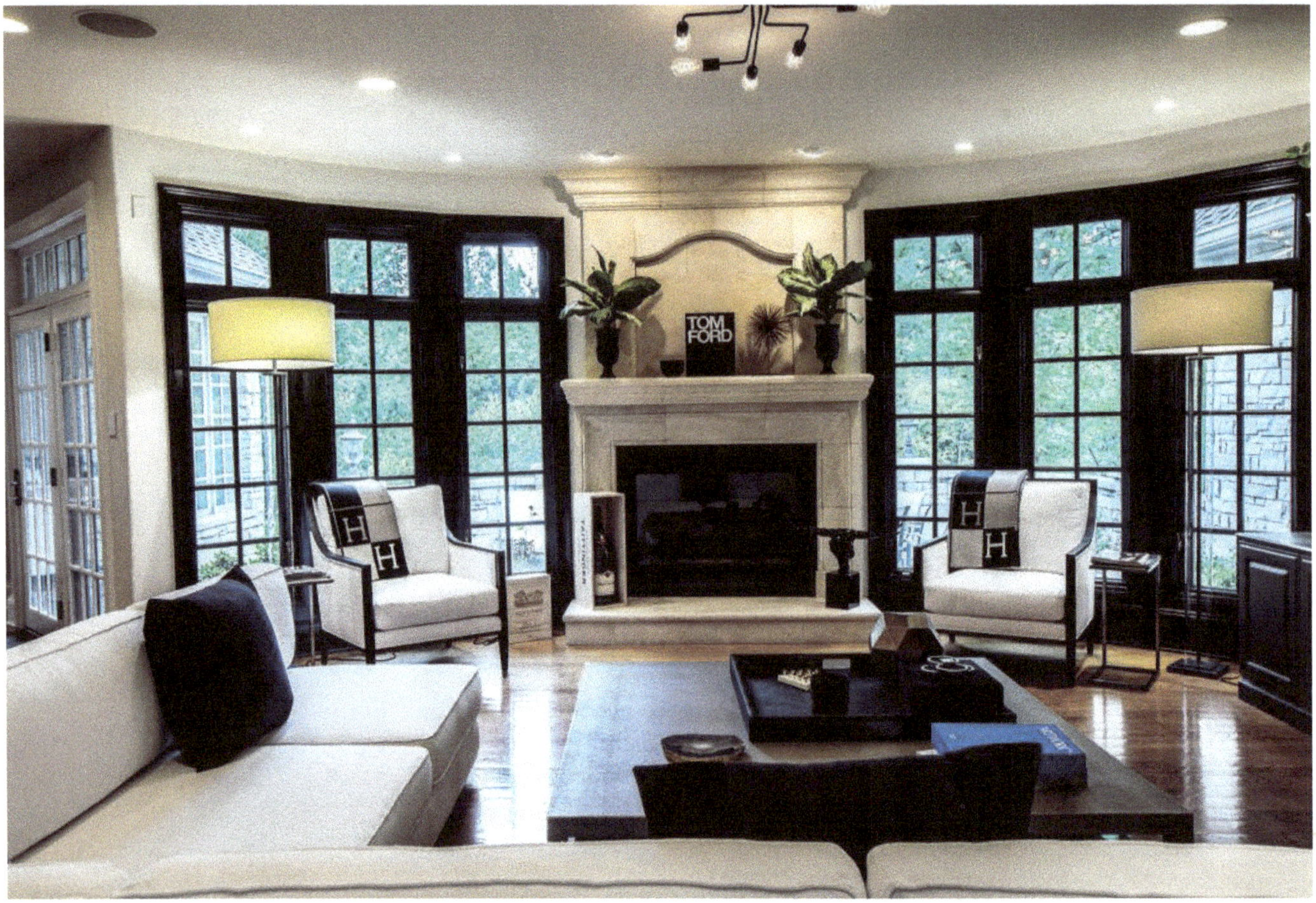
TOM
FORD

ABOVE: The incredible egg chairs were the starting point for this dramatic room, followed by the zebra-print rug. And because I wanted to make sure you could still see the zebra-print rug, I chose a Lucite coffee table so as to not obscure focus. Gold accents from the chairs inspired the mirror and chandelier.

FACING PAGE TOP: Low-profile furniture and transparent Lucite accents allow the spectacular view to command all the attention.

FACING PAGE BOTTOM: Sometimes a super simple change, like painting the window trim black, can have an incredible impact. This living room was a mix of wood tones before, so neutralizing one draws the eye to the fireplace and backyard beyond.
Photographs by Robin Subar
Interiors by Shannon Antipov Designs, Hinsdale, IL, page 391

BELOW: This waterfront home on the bay near Sarasota was the first Florida home for a New York executive's family. To help them embrace a less formal lifestyle, we took out a heavy Tuscan stone fireplace and created in its place a new wall with a gas fireplace surrounded by custom millwork. Now it's a relaxing entertaining space, complete with a mirrored bar cabinet in the corner and gorgeous views of the bay.

FACING PAGE TOP: The family room of the same house overlooks the pool and boat dock, and is now a wonderful, casual place to watch television and play games. Texture can add so much—here, the cocktail table is lacquered raffia topped with glass and the credenza is covered in beautiful mother of pearl, while the motorized window treatments are made of embroidered linen.

FACING PAGE BOTTOM: The blues and greens and creams of this downtown condo high-rise are inspired by its water view. We created a seamless transition between indoors and out. Once again, textures inspire interest: the striated velvet Kravet chairs contrast with the hammered brass and glass cocktail table, while the wall on the left is covered in sparkling pieces of mica.
Photographs by Nicholas Ferris

Interiors by Collins Interiors, Longboat Key, FL, page 384

"Above all, there should be a commitment to beauty, elegance, and comfort."
—Barbara Gardner

ABOVE & RIGHT: The challenge of a large, rectangular living room is bringing intimacy and continuity to the expansive space. A grand Persian carpet unites the room and also serves as artwork on the floor. Sectional sofas are joined by organic-shaped low tables and accessory seating in the form of the undulating wooden wave bench and the deep teal ottomans. The middle of the room is accented by a vintage mirrored chest, which is striking against the clean, wood-paneled wall. Atop the chest sit a pair of Mexican papier-mâché dolls.

FACING PAGE TOP: The living room is a kaleidoscope of color, offset by the calm, neutral walls and orderly built-in bookshelves. The cozy, oversized sheepskin in front of the fireplace adds texture and warmth, while the two easily moveable felt ottomans provide flexible seating.

FACING PAGE BOTTOM LEFT: The international, well-traveled family has lived in London, New York, and Boulder and adventured throughout Europe, Africa, and Asia. As such, family photos, sculptural vases, and travel treasures are tucked in with the novels, biographies, and histories.

FACING PAGE BOTTOM RIGHT: Found locally, a bright blue hand-woven Afghan rug defines a small seating area connecting the living room and dining room.
Photographs by Heather Knierim/HBK Photography
Interiors by Jennifer Rhode Design, Boulder, CO, page 387

ABOVE: The owners of this home in Charlestown, Rhode Island, enjoy living in rhythm with their ocean surroundings and are mindful of preserving its natural beauty, so this renovation was exactly my kind of job. I try to incorporate elements of feng shui into my designs, and every element—wood, fire, earth, metal, and water—is represented here. We used a lot of natural materials such as grasses, wools, and linens, along with plenty of plants, to help the home sit within its environment. The home really reflects the owners' lifestyle, which is something I always try to capture.
Photographs by Michael Patrick Lefebvre
Interiors by Balanced Interiors, Narragansett, RI, page 383

BELOW TOP: Having been renovated into a year-round home, this 1930s beach house features an enlarged sunroom that can be enjoyed during every New England season. There are no window treatments to obstruct the east and south-facing views of the sunrise, gardens, and 100-year-old trees. The wood ceiling, coupled with the wood floor and wood trunk, is balanced by the metal umbrellas on the gable end—a feng shui element.

BELOW BOTTOM: In the same home, the big stone fireplace in the living room was one of the main reasons we didn't just knock everything down and start from scratch. Recognizing when a house has good bones, and what can be salvaged or repurposed, is very important in terms of living environmentally-conscious. I also believe that artwork is more important than most people realize. You could spend thousands on a countertop, but then hang a $50 print that brings the entire room down. Artwork that's framed behind glass bounces light and sound, so I encourage my clients to incorporate original artwork and support local artists whenever they can.
Photographs by Michael Patrick Lefebvre
Interiors by Balanced Interiors, Narragansett, RI, page 383

ABOVE: To keep the urban industrial loft feeling at this high-end residence in downtown Minneapolis, I focused on clean lines and sleek materials with the help of builder Revision LLC. The 72-inch ribbon fireplace is framed in textured metal and surrounded with floor-to-ceiling porcelain tile. The custom sectional and chairs were sourced from Italy, while sappy walnut floors and motorized roller shades complete the room.

FACING PAGE: Reclaimed wood salvaged from another project becomes the focal point in this rustic contemporary family room, built in partnership with Fred Nordahl Construction, Inc. It's complemented by dry-stacked ledge stone with a rockface mantel and hearth, all surrounding the 74-inch fireplace. The 14-foot custom sectional is a combination of leather and fabric, while art was commissioned to play off the warm earth tones in the room's color scheme.
Photographs by Alyssa Lee Photography
Interiors by M Gilbertson Design, Eden Prairie, MN, page 390

"Homeowners may not always have the vocabulary to articulate their vision. By using a technique called visual listening, we can look at images together to better interpret what they desire."
—Molly Gilbertson

BELOW TOP LEFT: My client loved her existing sofas so much she wouldn't buy this new home unless they would fit in the long, wide, contemporary living room—luckily, they did! They prove that classic pieces with great lines can work just about anywhere, from a traditional 1940s Southern home to a contemporary renovation.

BELOW TOP RIGHT: An abundance of white walls made art important in this home, as well as neutral-colored furnishings in family-friendly fabrics that could stand up to kids and a dog. Soft surfaces and splashes of color encourage playtime from both.

BELOW BOTTOM: Though the husband actively plays the grand piano, it wasn't the ultimate focal point in this double-sized living room. Book-matched quartzite slabs add interest without distracting from the incredible bayou views. The goal was a room that felt pleasant and full of light, but blended the two sides of the space and didn't compete with the windows.
Photographs by Julie Soefer
Interiors by Pamela Hope Designs, Houston, TX, page 390

ABOVE: This modern loft shares a refined collector's approach and a combination of tonal textures and color to create a sophisticated and easy vibe for city living. The open-concept loft was spatially planned to provide different usable living areas throughout. The lounge seating area has a low and comfortable sofa from RH, and the textural raw silk upholstered accent chairs are from Kelly Wearstler. The carved oak credenza, also from Kelly Wearstler provides a sculptural element to the space. The owner's collection of important mid century art and light fixtures bring a unique dialogue to the space that is as individual as the owner.

RIGHT: The dining room in this open loft features a space for the owner's cocktail bar, and a Le Corbusier chaise perfect for reading with the city views beyond. The custom bronze and fractured glass dining table and chairs were designed by Kelly Wearstler, while the antique bronze sculpture was found in a London antique store.
Photographs by Scott Gilbertson, AIA PSA Gilberston Photography, LLC
Interiors by Spencer Design Associates, Minneapolis, MN, page 391

"As a designer your most important pursuit is to bring your clients' vision and dreams to life, and sometimes that means bridging styles and periods and different tastes. That is the true craft of what we do."
—Shane Spencer

BELOW: What began as a standard design consultation ended in a significant structural remodel for Houston Astros manager A.J. Hinch and his family. Walls were moved to improve flow, counters and floors were replaced, and the addition of a new laundry enhances the home's functionality. A neutral color palette complemented by texture-rich finishes blends West Coast and Southern styles, creating a serene environment where this family on-the-go enjoys a daily dose of peace and relaxation.
Photograph by Julie Soefer

BELOW BOTTOM LEFT: These empty nesters love being outdoors, either nestled in the majestic courtyard or taking in the views from the beautiful yard. Their home is a play on bold patterns with thoughtful accents throughout—a classic design foundation with a fresh, modern feel.
Photograph by Carl Mayfield

BELOW BOTTOM RIGHT: Porches line the front and back of the home, with a ground-floor entertaining lounge, dining area, pool, boathouse, and shower. The entertaining space is comprised of the kitchen, dining room, living area, and 12-foot covered porch. Each area is seamless in its color scheme and provides a welcoming flow for guests.
Photograph by Colleen Duffley

Interiors by Melanie King Designs, The Woodlands, TX, page 389

ABOVETOP LEFT: When we worked with a young family in the Nashville suburb of Hendersonville, it was important to maintain the integrity of their midcentury modern home. This bonus room had a fire box, so we kept that idea and used the in-wall wood as a design element. The natural touch adds to the comfort of the space.

ABOVE TOP RIGHT: Set on historic Belmont Boulevard, this 1908 four-square home is as beautiful as it is fun. Because two young boys live here, we wanted them to feel welcome in every room—no space is off-limits. You'll notice the hopscotch rug, floor poofs, and wood floors that are ideal for skating and racing cars. The dining table was designed to take marks and scratches, blending them in to add to its patina.
This and above left photographs by Leslee Mitchell

ABOVE BOTTOM: This hip 1920s house in the 12 South neighborhood was bought by a young professional couple. We added about 2,800 square feet and made sure the family room suited them and their beloved dogs. We used a custom modular sofa and custom-built cabinets that conceal two large televisions—ideal for a couple who loves gaming and entertainment. An original painting from local artist Trevor and porcelain Daltile surround the fireplace.
Photograph by Reagen Taylor

Interiors by JL Design, Nashville, TN, page 387

ABOVE TOP: We redesigned a living room to provide a clean, contemporary aesthetic, adding a tasteful custom fireplace as the central point.
Photograph by Mike Duerinckx

ABOVE BOTTOM LEFT: Located waterside in Florida, this vacation escape is filled with festive colors. Whimsical coastal elements punctuate its Art Deco style.
Photograph by Mike Duerinckx

ABOVE BOTTOM RIGHT: My signature dramatic scale is emphasized in a modern living room space glamorously appointed with a show-stopping, floor-to-ceiling crystal chandelier.
Photograph by Tony Marinella

Interiors by Esther Boivin Interiors, Scottsdale, AZ, page 386

RIGHT: This traditional home in Great Falls, Virginia, received a complete revamp, giving it new—and stylish— life. Painting the faux wood beams black created a high contrast, and the draperies match the ceiling's stark geometry. Emerald accents deliver just the right amount of pop.

BELOW LEFT: The bay window area next to the kitchen used to have seating for four, but now it gets much more use as a lounge area. The kids kick their feet up on the chaises—blankets strategically keep the white upholstery clean—while Mom cooks, and everyone gets to enjoy the beautiful views outside. Now, the office across the hall has become the breakfast room and coffee bar, and everyone is much happier with the changes.

BELOW RIGHT: The living room became a purposeful space for relaxing and chatting in small groups by putting in chairs instead of one big sofa. The zebra "hide" rug is actually needlepoint, which gives it extra depth and originality.
Photographs by Stacy Zarin Goldberg
Interiors by GreyHunt Interiors, Chantilly, VA, page 387

ABOVE TOP: I'm originally from New Mexico, so I'm drawn to a combination of contemporary and rustic. That's apparent in the live-edge wood coffee tables by a local artisan David Alan, flanked by two leather club chairs from Pottery Barn. Four different colors of chiseled-edge limestone with a brushed finish give the floor movement and interest.

ABOVE BOTTOM: The homeowners wanted a bar area, so we optimized a small wall off the kitchen with a rustic china cabinet from Restoration Hardware, giving them a space to mix drinks while showcasing their glassware. Moving into the living room, all the elements work together: a leather sofa, linen pillows, and a reclaimed wood coffee table, utilizing natural materials to create a cozy living room.
Photographs by Micah Trostle, Trostle Films
Interiors by Designers i, San Diego, CA, page 385

BELOW TOP: The primary living space is more "within the roof" than any other, stepping up from the private sleeping spaces and collecting daylight and air from three sides, overseeing the long drive across the property. In the shared warmth of the slate fireplace, this is a space for reading and weaving.

BOTTOM: Woven between limestone hearth and farmhouse, the south sunroom is also a gateway to both house and site, at grade. Rustic stone underfoot precedes and exits the space, outdoors and undercover toward the river. Wood-framed compositions—painted, simple, and lightly adorned—also form the north primary bedroom suite.
Photographs by Andrea Rugg
Interiors by CF Design Ltd, Duluth, MN, page 384

ABOVE TOP: It was important to develop an industrial chic vibe in this condo at the historic Book Cadillac Hotel in downtown Detroit, honoring history with the client's family antiques while also honoring 21st-century craftsmanship. A vintage dining table and chairs, for example, is paired with Danish modern pieces that reference the heirlooms. Detroit-based Smithshop created a bespoke steel-and-brass room divider, which is filled with chicken-wire glass reclaimed from a warehouse in New York City.
Photograph by Gene Meadows

ABOVE BOTTOM: Joining two penthouse condo units together in Rosslyn, Virginia, presented a unique opportunity to create an elegant, light-filled home that incorporated the building's ductwork and structural masonry columns into the design. A custom hair-on-hide rug from Kyle Bunting grounds a classic Eames chaise and welcoming Minotti sofa and ottoman. The developer was going to cover up the brick, but there's something special about the elegance of the furnishings juxtaposed with the architecture's rougher materials.
Photographs by Stacy Zarin Goldberg
Interiors by Design Milieu, Washington, DC, page 385

ABOVE: This loft in River Oaks has a fabulous view of downtown Houston, but those lovely, huge windows could also make it glaringly hot. Motorized Lutron shades were the solution—this was the start of the homeowner's love of home automation—and they were the start of the living room's complete remodel. The owner already had a great deal of wonderful artwork, so we replaced the furniture to be more neutral and enlarged and reclad the fireplace with a wedge-shaped slate tile to ground the room.
Photograph by Miro Dvorscak
Interiors by Chandra Stone Interior Design, Houston, TX, page 384

ABOVE TOP LEFT: This living room design is framed by a 30-foot ceiling and arched wood-framed windows and doors, creating a dramatic statement of style and comfort. The limestone custom-carved fireplace is coordinated with leather and down-stuffed furnishings, while turquoise accents add depth and visual interest.
Photograph by INSPIRO 8 STUDIOS

ABOVE TOP RIGHT: The soaring ceiling of this lake house's living room is beautifully framed with reclaimed wood, specially selected to complement the stone accents. The room's focal point is the locally quarried stone fireplace, which immediately captures your attention thanks to the neutral furnishings and coordinating accessories that surround it.
Photograph by INSPIRO 8 STUDIOS

ABOVE BOTTOM: This contemporary styled living room is elegant and open, with a granite flush fireplace and uniquely "stepped design" mantel. Gold and brass trim, lighting, and accents gently lead your eye from one space to the next.
Photograph by Getz Images

Interiors by Ca'Shae Interior Design, Roswell, GA, page 383

ABOVE: Clean and crisp, this layout was designed to enhance the view of the outside. Though the palette is neutral, it's the different textures—leather, suede, Venetian plaster—that give it interest. The rug also adds movement to the room, with its hints of blue picking up on the blue tones that run throughout the home. Our in-house floral designer, Marilyn Brosang, creates arrangements that are more like sculptural pieces of art than traditional bouquets, and one of these is prominently displayed on the coffee table.
Photograph by Miro Dvorscak

Interiors by B. de Vine Interiors, Houston, TX, page 383

BELOW TOP: A palette of creams, whites, and blues create a breezy, airy vibe in a reimagined living room where guests can relax before moving into the adjacent dining room for holidays and dinner parties. Custom maps of sentimental locations, from college towns to annual vacation spots, add a beautifully personalized touch to the space.

BELOW BOTTOM: We continued the airy feeling into the dining room, with its subtly textured wallpaper and a statement mirror that bounces natural light around.
Photographs by Rebecca McAlpin Photography
Interiors by Glenna Stone Interior Design, Philadelphia, PA, page 386

BELOW TOP: This home underwent a full gut remodel, always with the intention to show off the homeowners' incredible art collection. Beautiful European oak floors and clean white walls do just that, providing the perfect backdrop. We added the custom, contemporary sectional sofa in a menswear-inspired tweed fabric for a timeless look. The ottoman was created with charcoal mohair and sexy acrylic legs to be sure that the vintage Turkish rug gets the attention it deserves.

BELOW BOTTOM: This modern home on Lake LBJ features the unique architectural detail of a floating staircase, while store-front windows capture all the natural light. The iconic mid-mod Noguchi table and clean-lined sectional both feature warm walnut to tie in the stair treads. A shag rug feels yummy underfoot, and the black leather recliner makes this a fabulous space to relax and revive.
Photographs by Danny Batista
Interiors by Abode Interior Design, San Antonio, TX, page 382

ABOVE: Elegant but comfortable, this living space is also open to the kitchen and dining rooms so it echoes their brass accents. The furnishings are all custom, with cozy touches like chairs that swivel for better conversation and monogrammed pillows for a personal touch. The insets of the coffered ceiling are wallpapered to further emphasize the architecture from Nations Homes, while the blue and cream color scheme ties into its coastal location.

LEFT: "Southern elegance" sums up this home, which despite its soaring coffered ceilings and expansive windows still feels cozy and intimate. The stone fireplace is a focal point in a space that's conducive to conversation.
Photographs by Scott Smallin
Interiors by Legacy Interiors, Myrtle Beach, SC, page 388

ABOVE: When we designed a loft in a historic building located in an artsy area of downtown Louisville, we started with the client's mix of traditional items, rustic furnishings, and modern art. Once a warehouse, the building now offers modern condos with features such as exposed brick and vent pipes—tons of character. We added to what the client already owned to accentuate her style, and selected furnishings that made sense for her busy life of work-related travel and her large, dark-haired German Shepherd.
Photograph by Accent Photography
Interiors by KP Designs, Louisville, KY, page 388

Laurie McRae Interiors, Augusta, GA, page 388

Kitchen Spaces

It's no wonder that kitchens are commonly named as the favorite room of the house. The space provides literal nourishment, as well as nourishment for the heart and soul. It's the room where you commune with family members and friends, and it offers a spot to decompress and share events of the day.

I consider a few key points when designing a kitchen, whether I'm working on a new build or renovation. Because it's vital to everyday activities, the kitchen has to function well and should be built specifically to fit the homeowners. Do they entertain? Are there young children? What are the ages and abilities of the family members? Are they foodies or oenophiles? Then I pinpoint who primarily cooks in the home and cater to that. The major prep area needs to be oriented toward the gathering space in the room or adjacent area, so that the cook never feels isolated or left out of activities.

The final thing I consider is what work space would serve the cook(s) best. Kitchen trends evolve, and recently families have moved from the kitchen triangle theory—with activity happening between the range, refrigerator, and sink—to a more linear concept. The work-station sink, which incorporates cutting boards, colanders, and accessories, has risen in popularity and changed the traditional work flow. These work-station sinks are typically located in a center island and allow several people to be involved in, or observant of, the cook's activities.

The most satisfied homeowners work with an interior designer to carefully consider these points, and balance the choice of appliances with their culinary level—all while considering budget and real estate prices. Kitchens must work on all levels to have a lasting appeal.

I hope you can pull inspiration from these pages, and that they might spark ideas for your own kitchens, or any room in your home.

Good luck!

Laurie McRae, NCIDQ, AKBD, GA Registered Interior Designer
Laurie McRae Interiors
Augusta, GA
see page 388

Gavin Green Home Design, page 386

GreyHunt Interiors, page 387

CF Interiors, page 384

BELOW & PREVIOUS PAGE: I love when a client shares his or her clear vision for a room—which is what gave us inspiration for this newly furnished collaboration. Along with the client, I worked closely with the architect and contractor to help the couple transition from traditional living to contemporary. The new kitchen is serene and uncluttered, with a place for everything. The walnut-panel wall secretly houses the pantry with all the small appliances and dry goods.
Photographs by Steve Bracci Photography
Interiors by Laurie McRae Interiors, Augusta, GA, page 388

ABOVE TOP: This kitchen was inspired by the homeowner's inherited primitive corner cupboard in the adjacent space. We pulled the finish of the wood into the hood, used an antique wall cabinet, and varied the heights of the cabinets for an unfitted look.

ABOVE BOTTOM: When we did a kitchen remodel for a couple with young kids, our biggest challenge was to create a small table next to the L-shaped island that was safe for the children to use. In order to make the table secure, we had to pull off an engineering feat. We pinned the table leg through the basement and also tapped through the glass from the top, then floated the glass on a tile edge and siliconed it to keep it in place. This makes an ideal study space that can be overseen by the cook. The lighting incorporates an antique pendant with contemporary fixtures, and well-placed task lighting.
Photographs by Steve Bracci Photography
Interiors by Laurie McRae Interiors, Augusta, GA, page 388

ABOVE: A galley kitchen set within a ranch-style home features plenty of midcentury nods and common-sense design. With no traditional wall cabinets, the champagne-stain, rift-cut vertical veneer storage is used for heavy plates and cookware, which makes lifting and moving items much easier. Focal points include the often-used chalkboard and the custom hood in a pale grey high-gloss paint. Although they require some extra maintenance, black Brazilian soapstone countertops add a beautiful dark layer against the white marble-stacked mosaic tile. The drawers designate work zones and help divvy up duties with multiple cooks in the kitchen.
Photographs by Robert Radifera
Interiors by Aidan Design, Silver Spring, MD, page 382

BELOW: This homeowner was looking for a classic, inviting kitchen with an edge so we incorporated a black, white, and gold palette. While balancing light and symmetry, we opened up the space and added two windows on either side of the range. The Wood-Mode full overlay door cabinets in Nordic white on maple, Carrara-honed marble countertops, and Suprema crystal white-gloss, brick-ceramic field tiles create a bright, clean setting, while the details add warmth. Satin brass bar pulls, Newport Brass plumbing fixtures, and a Circa Lighting Arabelle pendant light finish the space in style. For storage solutions, we took advantage of space in the dining room.
Photographs by Robert Radifera
Interiors by Aidan Design, Silver Spring, MD, page 382

ABOVE: Because the focal point of this empty nesters' home, located in a historic district, is the backyard with its lush gardens and pool, we added a large kitchen window which is flanked by aspect library sconces centered on the opening from the dining room, to take advantage of the views. In addition, the butler's pantry was expanded to serve as a daily breakfast bar for coffee and tea, while transitioning to a formal space for cocktails in the evening. A mixture of warm elements, including the Lewis Dolin satin brass pulls and glass round knobs on the Wood-Mode vintage Dover Cliffs maple cabinets, Rohl farmhouse sink, and Hansgrohe faucets, finish the space. Thibaut wallpaper and Pratt & Larson textured field tiles add to the kitchen's soft elegance. Urban Country counter stools pair beautifully with the knotty alder island.
Photographs by Robert Radifera
Interiors by Aidan Design, Silver Spring, MD, page 382

BELOW: Working in collaboration with Sally Steponkus Interiors, this classic tone-on-tone kitchen with custom light grey cabinets in Benjamin Moore's Smoke Embers is elevated by the eye-catching de Gournay hand-painted silk wallpaper backsplash. Richard Subaran on our team developed a creative solution for protecting the wallpaper by adding a tempered-glass overlay, which offers a refined, protective layer to this elegant finish. The dover door-style cabinetry features Brixton pulls in polished nickel, while the countertops are Caesarstone Frosty Carrina. The eat-in kitchen and dining room feature more formal lighting, including a traditional chandelier over the table, brass-accented pendants over the island, and wall sconces on each side of the window.
Photographs by Robert Radifera
Interiors by Aidan Design, Silver Spring, MD, page 382

BELOW: To begin this kitchen, we had to completely demolish what was originally there: an inefficient layout with minimal natural light. We took out a wall, reconfigured an entry closet, removed a door, closed the doorway, and enlarged the opening to the great room. These changes helped with the cramped space and feeling of isolation. Custom oak vertical-grain cabinets, Cinnamon Ice granite countertops, and natural britannium hardware give the kitchen its luxe look.

FACING PAGE: Originally a two-story space, this kitchen needed adequate lighting. In order to do that, we suspended circular, low-hanging pendants above the island.
Photographs by Jon Mancuso
Interiors by Lori Carroll & Associates, Tucson, AZ, page 389

117

BELOW & FACING PAGE BELOW: When we designed this kitchen in an architecturally traditional home, we knew the couple had a modern edge that should shine here. Traditional cabinet pulls and crackle-style subway tiles marry with the traditional architecture while being complemented by the contemporary accents. The custom hood has an eye-catching gold tuxedo stripe down the side. We opted for open shelves to lighten the room when too many traditional-style cabinets began to overwhelm the space. You can see the blend of traditional and modern, with classic cabinets and quartz counters featuring contemporary lighting and seating selections, easing into modern vibes. Fully remodeled and completely gutted, the kitchen originally had one large island, which was particularly troublesome for the not-so-tall lady of the house. The solution we arrived at was to turn it into two separate islands with distinct purposes. One is meant for cooking and features two dishwashers, while the other is meant for entertaining purposes and includes a wine fridge and icemaker.
Photograph by Lance Selgo, Unique Exposure Photography

FACING PAGE TOP: Family-friendly with plenty of sitting and serving space, this kitchen was remodeled and opened up into the main living area, where it had once been separated. We used a trio of glass globes so they don't interrupt sight lines yet still create a divider. The house has a black-accent scheme throughout, and the traditional hood here takes on a contemporary look with the deep color. Made of quartzite, the beautiful island counter has movement in the pattern, while the perimeter counter appears still and solid. Beneath the island countertop is a deep iron-ore color, which blends with the family room decor.
Photograph by Stratton Creative

Interiors by ML Interiors Group, Dallas, TX , page 389

*"Your house is the backdrop for your life.
Why not make it beautiful?"*
—Michelle Lynne

"Inspiration comes from my desire to make spaces not only beautiful to the eye, but beautifully functional for the ones who inhabit that space."
—Linda Knight Carr

BELOW: This small kitchen embodies light and sparkle. The island is designed for seating on one side and varied storage on the other. By design, there are no appliances on it; the island itself functions as a serving counter. Storage is a premium, so we maximized the space available with two cupboards flanking a built-in display cabinet for the clients' white pottery and sterling silver collection—which, when lit at night, becomes quite striking. The built-in cupboards were designed to precise scale and covered by a pair of 18th-century shutters. They display an original painting of urns and flowers and were the inspiration for the color palette and other elements in the space.
Photograph by Mark Salisbury

FACING PAGE: The kitchen's look, function, and special arrangement were paramount for a couple who loves to cook and eat. This architecturally contemporary home in Texas provided an opportunity to design floor-to-ceiling cabinetry with the emphasized beauty of the wood and the simplicity of the hardware. Natural stone countertops and backsplashes, plus light-tone floors, provide the contrast to the dark cabinets and define a subtle geometry within the space. Clear glass shows off a few of the client's favorite pieces while etched glass allows others to be present but not studied.
Photograph by Jake Holt
Interiors by Knight Carr & Company, Greensboro, NC, Page 388

ABOVE, FACING PAGE TOP & BOTTOM LEFT: This young couple's dream home had two specific criteria: be open to nature and support a professionally trained home chef. Positioning the range on the island allows her to face her guests as she's cooking, while the wall of windows practically erases the barrier between indoors and out. The island's waterfall edge enhances the inherent movement in the stone slab, and the navy cabinets feel traditional yet fresh.

FACING PAGE BOTTOM RIGHT: To up the drama in the wet bar off the kitchen, we fashioned a backsplash entirely out of antique mirrored glass. The soaring ceilings initially posed a challenge for lighting, but with the help of builder Scott Daves Construction we created a plan with fixtures placed just so to create a functional and beautifully layered look.
Photographs by Dustin Peck Photography
Interiors by Southern Studio, Cary, NC, page 391

*"We are surrounded by design inspiration every single day,
if you just know where to look."*
— Vicky Serany

ABOVE TOP LEFT: Art was the key component here. Because the home belongs to an art collector, we wanted the contemporary paintings to take center stage. A metal hood, a wall of glass cabinets, and sleek base cabinets complete the modern appeal.
Photograph by Brie Williams Photography

ABOVE TOP RIGHT & BOTTOM LEFT: This kitchen is great for entertaining and features top-of-the-line appliances, a comfortable breakfast room, and ample catering space. With southern exposure, the room floods with natural light during the day, but nighttime presented a challenge. The vaulted ceiling creates a vast space, so we took a tiered approach with large sculptural globes, sconces, and monopoint lights.
Photographs by Dustin Peck Photography

ABOVE BOTTOM RIGHT: Entertaining is simple with a living space like this, as it's an extension of the pool area. The bar is a comfortable spot to relax indoors for a moment and enjoy a drink or grab a bite to eat without leaving the party.
Photograph by Jane Beiles Photography
Interiors by Design Lines Signature, page 385

BELOW: We focused on efficiency as much as we did aesthetics with the fully remodeled space. The professional-grade range, pizza oven, and island refrigeration make the kitchen a dream to cook in. It's roomy without being too big and shows off the clean look of black and white subway tiles, with grey, silver, and white tones.
Photograph by Jane Beiles Photography
Interiors by Design Lines Signature, Page 385

LEFT: For homeowners who love to cook, we went up with the ceiling during the kitchen's full remodel, and made space to showcase the copper cookware. The client is from Alaska and wanted a nod to the outdoors. We used natural elements, such as the live-edge wood table, to capture an organic feel.
Photograph by Dustin Peck

BOTTOM LEFT: We reimagined a kitchen after the home had been hit by massive flooding. The simple yet elegant space has an Asian flair throughout, including the brass light fixtures.
Photograph by Robert Clark

FACING PAGE TOP LEFT: French interiors meet Virginia-style farmhouse in this Orlando home. The chef's kitchen features reclaimed beams brought in from the homeowner's personal farm.
Photograph by Robert Clark

FACING PAGE TOP RIGHT: Set on a marsh, this Beaufort, South Carolina, home shows off elements of its site. Aquatic tones and a teakwood ceiling offer a connection to the environment.
Photograph by Robert Clark

BELOW: The homeowner is a baker and we designed this kitchen with that in mind. It was a complete remodel so everything was customized to suit her needs, including plenty of counter space and top-of-the-line appliances.
Photograph by Robert Clark

Interiors by LGB Interiors, Columbia, SC, page 389

BELOW: Steeped in history, this late-1800s home needed an overhaul. The original enclosed kitchen was designed for staff, with a service staircase leading to the upper floors. Removing the staircase grew the kitchen by 50 feet, providing ample space for a massive kitchen island and a modern layout. The new kitchen reflects a classic black and white color palette with a jolt of color from the crimson Jean De Merry Lumiere chandelier. Classic soapstone is used throughout, with beveled subway tiles wrapping the walls. French limestone in an ebonized finish was placed on the diagonal to bring movement and flow to the floor. Bertoia barstools add just the right contemporary touch.
Artwork by Ryan Oreweiler
Photographs by Daniel Feldkamp
Interiors by Spencer Design Associates, Minneapolis, MN, page 391

ABOVE: Classic Shaker cabinetry in a stunning custom shade of the deepest blue is coupled with matte black accents in the La Cornue range and hood and burnished brass handmade hardware from England. The island was created at two heights so the owners could comfortably cook together; the lower island waterfalls with the Cambria quartz, while the upper portion has a custom walnut plank butcher block counter. The owners are also wine collectors, so a custom, 12-foot-high, temperature-controlled wine cellar was crafted in Sonoma County and transported to Minnesota to prominently display their collection.
Artwork from Art Resources Gallery
Photographs by Scott Gilbertson, AIA, PSA Gilbertson Photography, LLC
Interiors by Spencer Design Associates, Minneapolis, MN, Page 391

ABOVE TOP: We chose a fresh, light palette that gave the previously dark and dated kitchen a brighter, more timeless feeling. A larger quartzite slab on the island allowed for three new counter stools and extra casual seating.

ABOVE LEFT: A custom banquette along with new built-ins and cabinetry anchored the breakfast nook, which doubles as a work-from-home location during the day.

ABOVE RIGHT: The custom cabinet color is a neutral, almost white, tone that, when paired with the lightly crackled subway tile, keeps the kitchen light and airy and maximizes the natural light from the windows at either end of the kitchen.
Photographs by Rebecca McAlpin Photography
Interiors by Glenna Stone Interior Design, Philadelphia, PA, page 386

BELOW TOP: The juxtaposition of rustic hewn beams against the crisp white custom cabinetry makes a strong statement, while leathered blue quartzite tops the counters on both islands for a blend of visual and tactile texture.

BELOW BOTTOM: The hand-cut stained glass mosaic-tile backsplash serves as the focal point for the entire space, and was a key element in the design concept.
Photographs by Rebecca McAlpin Photography
Interiors by Glenna Stone Interior Design, Philadelphia, PA, page 386

ABOVE TOP LEFT: Unexpected flashes of shine can be found in this remodeled kitchen, from bits of mirror in the chevron-tiled backsplash to the stainless steel drawers next to the cooktop.

ABOVE TOP RIGHT: One way to achieve a family-oriented, warm feeling is by painting the cabinets a happy blue. The wood floors and bamboo shades balance out the bold color.

ABOVE BOTTOM LEFT: Giving a pop of color and expensive look (on a budget) is the contrasting fabric on the back of the barstools and pretty pattern that the tile is set.

ABOVE BOTTOM RIGHT: We kept the historic home's remodel feeling appropriate with little details like the turned legs on the island, traditional faucets, and printed concrete tile backsplash. The inside of the cabinets is painted the same color as the island to make it reminiscent of a china cabinet.
Photographs by Jessie Preza
Interiors by Lisa Gielincki Interior Design, Jacksonville, FL, page 389

BELOW TOP: This cross-grain mahogany cabinetry is full of hidden compartments, including the fridge and appliances. The hood is tiled with textured large-format tile, the same as the backsplash, to blend seamlessly.

BELOW BOTTOM: Another instance where I painted the inside of cabinets the same color as island, which—along with the cast stone hood and patterned backsplash—provide the traditional feel that's balanced by the modern commercial appliances.
Photographs by Jessie Preza
Interiors by Lisa Gielincki Interior Design, Jacksonville, FL, page 389

ABOVE: With 180-degree views of downtown Dallas, the high-rise apartment has a layout that resulted from the merging of two units. This is what makes it such a distinct space, but also what made it a challenge. We included a custom built-in breakfast table for an informal dining space that would also capitalize on the sweeping view. Top-hinged Redstone cabinetry and stainless-steel Porcelanosa tile are the highlights of the kitchen.
Photograph by Christian Sykora—The Full Package Media Team

FACING PAGE TOP: We completely refashioned this space to give a traditional home the kitchen it deserves. Refaced drawers, painted cabinetry, and a customized Vent-A-Hood transformed the room. Under-lit semi-precious quartz counters and the quartzite bar top add luxury to the busy family kitchen.
Photograph by Maksimilian Lab

FACING PAGE BOTTOM: Budget-friendly projects can look high-end by blending reasonably priced items with a few designer elements. We mixed builder-grade kitchen features and light fixtures from Wayfair with custom Redstone cabinets in a high-lacquer finish, marble and brass tile, and designer hardware that stands out.
Photograph by Miriam Hill

Interiors by Total 360 Interiors, Dallas, TX, Page 392

"Wood, textures, pops of color, and patterns keep spaces interesting and comfortable, even in the most modern of designs."
—Kat Black

LEFT, BELOW & FACING PAGE: When we designed this kitchen, we accommodated the husband and wife's separate requests. As the main cook, she wanted her work spaces open and clear of grazers. We expanded the room by four feet and moved the refrigerator away from her prep area. This let us add a wine serving and tasting area, which is what the husband wanted. We moved the cooktop to a long wall to maximize space and to serve as a focal point, and augmented the island, moving all seating to one side.

"Fantasy Black Leather" was used to fabricate the plant trough behind the sink, as well as all countertops and surfaces. The backsplash is hand-glazed subway tile and an elongated hexagon shape was used with the same finish for a subtle accent at the cooktop. Designed by Vermont's Simon Pearce, the light fixture serves as functional art in the room. Repurposed wood beams became display shelves at the beverage center, "legs" on the island, and supports for the custom range hood and corbels. Virginia Cabinetry matched that wood for three sides of the island and for the wine storage cabinets at the top of the beverage center.

Photographs by Quentin Penn-Hollar, QPH Photo
Interiors by Kathy Corbet Interiors, Richmond, VA, page 387

BELOW & FACING PAGE: The kitchen and dining spaces have an understated beauty and classic appeal. Clean lines and natural materials make for a serene setting. Because we made sure that ocean views were present from every room, the homeowners get the unique experience of observing nature throughout the day. One majestic encounter that they shared was seeing a small pod of whales feeding at the ocean's surface. They witnessed whales rise above the water as they lunged for their food, sometimes coming out vertically for a
Architect: Daniel Fletcher / Architects PC
Photographs by Aaron Leitz Photography
Interiors by Carson Guest, Atlanta, GA, page 384

"I love spaces that are simple enough to be calm and soothing, and not too busy. A home should be a retreat, a comfort to the soul."
—Rita Carson Guest

ABOVE TOP: A traditional kitchen with custom wood features allows the patterned tile backsplash to shine. The range hood mantel, sink valance, and concealed dishwasher and refrigerator panels are clever ways to give the room cohesion. Choosing solid cherry for the island provides a nice contrast to the white cabinetry painted in Sherwin Williams Dover White.
General contracting by Quality West Construction, Inc.

ABOVE BOTTOM: Natural walnut cabinets complement the ceiling beams in this country estate, which has room to entertain and then some. The cabinets also act as a beautiful contrast to the hickory flooring, quartz countertops, and tile backsplash.
Collaboration with Laurie Driscoll Interiors, general contracting by Quality West Construction, Inc.
Photographs by Marcia Hansen Photographic Company
Interiors by Curran Cabinetry & Design, Madison, WI, page 385

BELOW TOP: Custom wine racks and extended island seating make this sleek kitchen an entertainer's dream. A soft contemporary palette of white and grey comes through in the tile backsplash and veined quartz counters, with the cabinets painted in Sherwin Williams Extra White for the perimeter and Grizzly Grey for the island.
General contracting by Thiede Construction.
Photograph by Marcia Hansen Photographic Company

BELOW BOTTOM: Large windows and painted cabinets in soft, neutral colors brighten the farmhouse kitchen space and provide views to the outdoors. The cabinets are done in Sherwin Williams Unusual Grey and the island shade is Night Owl.
Collaboration with Fig Interiors
Photograph by S. Cole Photography

Interiors by Curran Cabinetry & Design, Madison, WI, page 385

ABOVE: This unique kitchen was made for a young bachelor in an up-and-coming area. With entertaining at the forefront of its design, the kitchen features a 60-inch garage-door window that raises at the touch of a button to reveal a bar ledge on the other side. The cabinets are true acrylic and have the same finish you'd find on a sports car, offering a high-gloss, reflective look. A couple of places show off under-lit elements, including the island's overhang and the custom cabinets.
Photograph by Leslee Mitchell

FACING PAGE BOTTOM: This kitchen was a new build in Green Hills for a young professional family who often hosts parties and get-togethers. With three kids, the homeowners needed a functional space that also prioritizes entertaining. The layout includes a butler's pantry, Sub-Zero and Wolf appliances—including the freezer, refrigerator, and wine tower—plus natural Calcutta marble countertops and European inset cabinets.
Photograph by Reagen Taylor
Interiors by JL Design, Nashville, TN, page 387

BELOW TOP LEFT: The architect on this home prioritized symmetry, and we honored that in our design. The skylights let natural light pour in and show off the contrast of light and dark finishes. Deep and spacious, the rift-cut oak island has a waterfall edge while the upper cabinets are free of hardware to accentuate the lines of the space.
Photograph by Reagen Taylor

BELOW TOP RIGHT: We refreshed a home on Belmont Boulevard that needed new vibes and fresh energy. The house is on the National Registry of Historic Places and has some beautiful vintage features from its turn-of-the-century beginnings that we preserved. We added Lucite chairs, hand-cut globe fixtures, vertical-glass mosaic tile above the range, and dark blue hues.
Photograph by Leslee Mitchell
Interiors by JL Design, Nashville, TN, page 387

BELOW: A clean, contemporary, tropical Asian-inspired look was achieved through the use of dark woods for the floor and cabinets, white quartz surfaces, glass fixtures, glass door cabinets, and complementary paint. The client's beautiful garden outside is the visual centerpiece, so wider windows and a serving pass-through were installed to visually and physically connect the kitchen to the backyard. The existing appliance wall was extended to compensate for lost storage space, while a cooking island with seating was added to improve the workflow.
Photographs by Mark Gebhardt, Mark Gebhardt Photography
Interiors by Raashi Design, San Ramon, CA, page 390

ABOVE TOP: This kitchen and bar were designed as a great entertaining space, with the bar counter's seating and storage—complete with a wine cooler—proving both fun and functional. The island features both induction and gas cooking, while the linear glass mosaic backsplash adds a bit of glimmer. This easy-maintenance kitchen is completed with an engineered quartz countertop, brushed nickel and stainless steel fixtures, and a copper bar sink.

ABOVE BOTTOM: A custom pass-through window and counter connect the kitchen and backyard, allowing the host to easily handle large parties, while the dropped ceiling and accent lighting add visual interest. The materials, fixtures, and design details make this a highly functional cook's kitchen.
Photographs by Dean J. Birinyi, Dean J. Birinyi Photography
Interiors by Raashi Design, San Ramon, CA, page 390

ABOVE & FACING PAGE: I designed this fresh and classic kitchen around a treasured piece of artwork the clients had, which influenced the navy island. The subway tile seems traditional, but there's a faint crackle to it that imparts a modern edge. Wide-plank white porcelain tile echoes the large apron sink—which we call a Belfast sink in Ireland. Because everything was so neutral, I wanted custom pendants that popped, and there's a larger, matching white one hanging over the dining table.
Photograph by Suzy Gorman

FACING PAGE RIGHT: The weightiness of the steel pulls balances the satin matte maple slab cabinet doors, which almost look like furniture. This kitchen is a mix of midcentury modern with traditional, and a hint of Asian through the 3-D tiles that are laid to resemble origami. The clients did not want glass shelving, so I developed a lighting system to run behind each exposed shelf so that the light would wash over their plates and glassware.
Photographs by Joel Marion

Interiors by Ash Leonard Design, St. Louis, MO, page 382

LEFT: At first glance, this one-of-a-kind mounted wine rack looks more like art than storage. It provides a beautiful and functional backdrop for the contemporary bistro table and acrylic chairs with brass frames.
Photograph by Getz Images

BOTTOM LEFT: This amazing lake home kitchen would please any five-star chef. Its 30-foot ceiling frames two spacious Islands and a gourmet stove accented with locally quarried stone. The rich walnut cabinetry blends beautifully with the timber-framed ceiling and wood plank-style accent wall.
Photograph by INSPIRO 8 STUDIOS

BOTTOM RIGHT: The combination of deep grey, soft white, and rich walnut in this transitional kitchen is elegant and inviting. Dramatic A-frame beams accentuate the 20-foot-high ceiling, and the room is grounded with dark wide-plank flooring. The oversized island provides ample seating and a built-in bookcase for extra storage.
Photograph by Getz Images

FACING PAGE TOP: Italian-inspired touches inform this spacious kitchen, with its ceiling-height cabinetry and arched trim. Two handcrafted wrought-iron chandeliers add Old World charm with soft candle lighting. The backsplash is reminiscent of a vintage Italian kitchen, keeping the space soft and inviting.
Photograph by INSPIRO 8 STUDIOS

FACING PAGE BOTTOM: Eye-catching gold and brass accents—such as the custom-crafted oven hood and hand-forged barstools—are used sparingly to keep the design of this condo kitchen interesting. The crystal hanging pendants provide light for the oversized island while looking like jewels as they sparkle above the fabulous quartz countertop.
Photograph by Getz Images
Interiors by Ca'Shae Interior Design, Roswell, GA, page 383

"The focus shouldn't only be on creating a beautiful and practical space, but also making sure everyone is happy each step of the way."
— Aven Kaga

FACING PAGE: A full-height white marble backsplash and custom painted white cabinetry have stood the test of time because of their clean and fresh look. Silver cabinet door trims, a stainless steel cooktop, silver circular chandeliers, and gold leaf counter stool tops create shadow details and layers of contrast that give the L-shaped white kitchen counter depth and lasting architectural interest.

BELOW: This white transitional kitchen achieves an immaculate and pristine appearance. The space features a marble backsplash, a solid white kitchen countertop, white painted Shaker-style cabinets, custom-made dining chairs with contrast color welts, and an adjustable solid maple wood table. Blue/grey furniture and trims keep the classic white space in balance.
Photographs courtesy of GAVIN GREEN HOME DESIGN LLC
Interiors by GAVIN GREENE HOME DESIGN LLC, page 386

"Considering the client and the designer, one might think that it takes merely 'two to tango,' until we also consider the composers, the musicians, the circle of admirers, the polisher of the floor, the dresser.... and the grower of the single red rose. The creative process is a celebration of teamwork."
—Cheryl Fosdick

BELOW TOP: This 14-foot-wide bridge between public and private domains is a true pavilion, both a refuge and an invitation. In a damp forest underlain with sandstone along Lake Superior, it is a constant play of light and air throughout the day, as the saturated ferns below drain uninterupted to the lakeshore.

BELOW BOTTOM: Inspired by rural French homesteads, the centerpiece of this new home is a limestone farmhouse with openings detailed in recycled oak, whose primary floor places the structured kitchen, with lofted bedrooms above, between two light-filled volumes of living and dining. The views are centered on a courtyard fountain and the river's edge peninsula.

FACING PAGE: Since its 1925 construction, this house has transformed décor often. Today, with layers of questionable trends removed, peacefulness, simplicity, and balance tell the story of community and home.
Photographs by Andrea Rugg
Interiors by CF Design Ltd, Duluth, MN, page 384

RIGHT, BELOW & FACING PAGE BOTTOM: Dani Harris' inspiration for this modern kitchen came from adding striking details and clean lines, mainly through Calacatta quartz. The veining continues into a thicker dropped-down edge in the island, and is carried up through the backsplash. Pieces of chrome in the faucet, legs, chandelier, and pulls add a pop of contrast. All these little details complete a beautiful, modern look.
Photographs by Amber Brooks, 87 Orange

FACING PAGE TOP: Cate Ball was inspired to transform this space into a calm and collected neutral haven that is both comfortable and inviting. The dining area is open to the kitchen, and the fireplace creates a cozy retreat. Silly family framed photos show the owners' sense of fun, but the room remains timeless and will surely be enjoyed for years to come.
Photograph by Troy Vanlangen, Above the Horizon Media
Interiors by Delight in Designs, Grand Rapids, MI, page 385

RIGHT & BELOW: As victims of a California wildfire, these homeowners left for work one day and came back to find their house completely gone. They were starting over with literally nothing, and we recreated a home for them centirely from scratch. Natural materials were a major influence, with warm woods providing the base for the kitchen. Putting the wine fridge on the side of the island is a clever use of space. This was unlike any other project I've done, and it was heartwarming to turn such a horrible event into something beautiful for their family.

FACING PAGE: My 1970s-era home in La Jolla has a midcentury modern vibe, but we updated the closed-in floorplan so that the kitchen and living room could be connected. I love natural stones and woods, so I chose a limestone floor and rift oak cabinets with two different stains. The countertops and backsplash are a natural quartzite stone with a honed finish. The fireplace is positioned between the kitchen and living room and was originally faced with white cinder block. It is certainly the focal point of the space, so we widened it on either side and faced it with large-format black porcelain tile, then hung a large chandelier by Visual Comfort in front to brighten it up. A rolling island in the middle of the kitchen has so many uses, including holding cheese platters and being rolled into the living room while entertaining.
Photographs by Micah Trostle, Trostle Films
Interiors by Designers i, San Diego, CA, page 385

ABOVE: In "horse country," traditional design reigns—though there are definitely opportunities to include a modern flourish here and there. We worked with the architect of Norris Architecture and kitchen designer Joey Olson on this charming Middleburg home that is welcoming and functional. Drink drawers next to the fridge are topped by a coffee bar, while double ovens handle the load of cooking for four kids and plenty of parties. A pot filler above the range was a must. Through a pocket door is an art studio with its own fireplace, along with a walk-in pantry containing another fridge, prep space, and plenty of storage.

FACING PAGE TOP & BOTTOM LEFT: Regina Andrews light fixtures are a focal point in what used to be a very dated, closed-in kitchen. We worked with the kitchen designers to include multiple countertop levels and open up the space—large enough to where the new hood didn't seem imposing. The purple textile accents play off the veining in the marble and soften the overall look. The gold bridge Brizo faucet ties in beautifully with the lighting and other finish details.

FACING PAGE BOTTOM RIGHT: Storage was a major priority, so a wall of built-ins was installed but practically disappeared thanks to the matching fridge and pantry fronts. A glimmering visual triangle of gold is created by the Hudson Valley lights, Brizo kitchen faucet, and barstools.
Photographs by Stacy Zarin Goldberg
Interiors by GreyHunt Interiors, Chantilly, VA, page 387

"There is power behind your environment. Changing your space can truly change your life for the better."
—Sallie J. Lord

BELOW: One of two kitchens in this coastal home gave a nod to its beach location with a watery blue island and the sculpture that sits atop it, called *Mermaid Under the Sea*. All of the intricate cabinets are custom-made, with a few glass fronts to show off beautiful pieces and antique mirrors to highlight the refrigerator.
Built by Babb Custom Homes.

FACING PAGE TOP: There are no drapes in this kitchen so as not to obstruct the view of the Intracoastal Waterway. I mixed a lot of blonde and brass finishes in this house, such as the statement-making brass light fixtures. Luxe touches, like custom cabinets and high-end appliances, elevate the space.

FACING PAGE BOTTOM: Inspired by an Italian house that the homeowner loves, this kitchen recreates the feel with oil paintings and layered draperies. Rich wood cabinets and an attached breakfast room create a gorgeous environment for this Southern gourmet cook.
Photographs by Scott Smallin
Interiors by Legacy Interiors, Myrtle Beach, SC, page 388

"The foundation of great design is open communication and a relentless focus on the details."
–Lucy Emory Hendricks

TOP & ABOVE LEFT: As lovers of vintage, the owners of this North Austin home wanted a simple canvas that would complement their ever-growing collection of artifacts. We kept the main living areas light and airy with a mix of light grey paint and white brick walls, and pops of color coming through in furniture, rugs, art, and light fixtures. The style of the home can best be described as modern meets vintage, with a minimal approach to decoration—just enough, and not too cluttered.
Photographs by Chase Daniel

ABOVE RIGHT: Peacock-blue lower cabinets and brass hardware don't feel overwhelming thanks to handmade white subway tiles and a mix of white upper cabinets and open shelving made from reclaimed wood.
Photograph by Sarah Natsumi Moore
Interiors by Urbane Design, Austin, TX, page 392

BELOW: To accommodate a busy family of four, the design of this home needed to be clean, clutter-free, and functional. We chose a classic meets contemporary style and used a neutral color palette filled with whites and greys to bring a light airiness to the home. We laid crisp subway tile as the backsplash and installed a stunning grey marble island with an undermount sink and built-in side cabinets. A sleek, custom, stainless steel vent hood accentuates the cooking area, creating the perfect space for cooking and hosting dinner parties.
Photographs by Chase Daniel
Interiors by Urbane Design, Austin, TX, page 392

BELOW TOP: We had several priorities when we designed this kitchen: satisfy the needs of a gourmet cook, preserve views of the mountains, provide for large informal gatherings, and create a warm contemporary environment. Under-counter storage allows for window walls and maintains openness. The cabinetry is quarter-fumed red gum and countertops are leathered granite. A contemporary-styled island combines custom acacia wood butcher block with finished metal table top and shelves.

BELOW BOTTOM: Here we used a large, multi-functional island to provide a casual, inviting space to cook, talk, and enjoy meals. The windows offer expansive views of the desert and allow homeowners to experience the outdoors from every angle.
Photographs by Kurt Munger
Interiors by Celaya | Soloway Interiors, Tucson, AZ, page 384

BELOW TOP: This couple's forever home is oriented around family—they have several grandchildren who visit often—so it was important that no room felt too shut off. Widening the doorway to the dining room and adding a huge island makes everything feel more welcoming, as does the cozy fireplace with marble surround. Their son-in-law is an architect, and the decorative support beams were his idea.

BELOW BOTTOM: Black, white, and lots of texture inform the kitchen of this brand-new construction about 25 minutes south of Austin. The husband is an artist—he contributed the stained wood vent hood and was very hands-on about the building details. Two different patterns of handmade, hand-glazed terra cotta tile were chosen for the backsplash, complementing the black-and-white veined silestone countertops. Another of my companies, Troo Design, specializes in cabinetry, so we constructed all the storage here.
Photographs by Keith Trigaci
Interiors by Patrice Rios Interiors, Austin, TX, page 390

ABOVE & LEFT: Our clients were looking for Old World appeal with a modern twist, so we found the perfect color combination for them. The effect of the color palette is quite glamorous when subtle variations of grey are layered with beautiful, bold touches of gold. With this, we achieved an elegant and straightforward look while also considerably dialing up the sophistication.
Photographs by Realty Pro Shots
Interiors by Susan Semmelmann Interiors, Fort Worth, TX, page 392

TOP LEFT: Keeping natural elements and colors were paramount in this home, which overlooks the bay. The beautiful veining of the Calcutta stone is the centerpiece of this kitchen, where a good amount of entertaining occurs.
Photograph by Colleen Duffley

TOP RIGHT: To accommodate a large family and lots of gatherings, the ample cabinetry was carefully thought out, while a clean glazed brick forms the backsplash and stainless steel details are tied into the hood. The wide oak flooring goes throughout the home and was stained to match driftwood from the beach. Soft linen drapery with silver stitching was used along the entire back wall of this level.
Photograph by Colleen Duffley

ABOVE: To add an edge to this kitchen, a geometric Phillip Jeffries wallcovering on the walls and ceiling of the desk area is combined with the full slab backsplash and clean lines. Key features such as the custom stainless hood and lighting used in both spaces lift the eye upwards.
Photograph by Julie Soefer
Interiors by Melanie King Designs, The Woodlands, TX, page 167

BELOW TOP LEFT: With a midcentury vibe and less-than-ideal 1970s décor, this home was very specific to its original owner. However, its current family had lived in New York City and Amsterdam and preferred clean, European design. We paired a large format terrazzo-style tile with Thermador appliances, modern white cabinets, and built-in breakfast nook with a turquoise upholstered banquette. The classic tulip table's chic profile is highlighted by the large window behind it.

BELOW TOP RIGHT: A young legal professional had purchased a high-end luxury townhome that was monochromatic in grey and white—this contrasted with her colorful, bohemian style. The kitchen was nicely appointed but needed a pop of color. Satin brass, pink, and white barstools do just that, making the space timeless and fun.

BELOW BOTTOM: We had just finished a complete renovation project with our clients when they called me to look at this townhome. It was a mish-mash of the worst of everything '80s, but the Buffalo Bayou location in one of Houston's best neighborhoods made it irresistible. We were able to appeal to their midcentury preferences thanks to the townhome's good bones. The seating nook and updated fireplace accented with Jonathan Adler pottery furthered the cool factor. There wasn't really room for a breakfast table and extra seating, but a perpendicular dropdown island created an eat-in kitchen while still feeling spacious.

Photographs by Julie Soefer
Interiors by Pamela Hope Designs, Houston, TX, page 390

ABOVE TOP: Symmetry looks even more inviting with a crisp white color palette and double islands, with the marble's veining adding a natural sense of movement.
Photograph by John Bessler

ABOVE BOTTOM: Always the "homiest" room in an apartment, the kitchen is a true gathering spot. Built-in seating gives everyone a room at the table, whether it's for dining, doing homework, or just having a conversation.
Photographs by Regan Wood
Interiors by Elissa Grayer Interior Design, Rye, NY, page 386

BELOW TOP: This modular Vipp kitchen is all steel construction with stainless countertops, sitting atop end-grain oak flooring. Smithshop masterfully executed a wall of hand-hammered brass tiles, each hung with brass tacks.
Photograph by Gene Meadows

BELOW BOTTOM: Small but efficient, this custom maple kitchen is laid out in sections to accommodate its unique floorplan. The refrigerator and built-in ovens are across from each other at the end of the galley section. The soapstone countertops wrap around into the dining room to provide a wet bar and seating area. Stainless steel mosaic tile shimmers behind floating shelves for the owners' collection of liqueurs.
Photograph by Stacy Zarin Goldberg

Interiors by Design Milieu, Washington, DC, page 385

BELOW TOP: Blue is not typically a color that's used in kitchens, but the cobalt island ended up being a beautiful focal accent to the vintage light fixtures, floating shelves, and butcher block counter. The ceiling beam indicates where the kitchen and dining room were originally separated. The coffee bar offers a separate space to prepare drinks, with the blackboard acting as ever-changing décor.

BELOW BOTTOM: High-rises typically have a vertical utility pipe that can be difficult to deal with—instead of it being a challenge, I encased it in a column that showcases the owner's prized teapot from Turkey. Macaubas quartzite for the extra-long island adds a sense of movement, while all outlets are hidden under the upper cabinets so as not to disturb the seamless look of the glass backsplash.
Photographs by Miro Dvorscak
Interiors by Chandra Stone Interior Design, Houston, TX, page 384

ABOVE: Transforming a heavy brown, burgundy, and gold-colored kitchen to a modern masterpiece is a D'KOR HOME by Dee Frazier Interiors favorite, and the perfect space to cook those new recipes the client has been wanting to tackle. New, bright white custom cabinets and hues of blue, green, and violet, accented with silver metallics, strike the perfect balance of transitional and contemporary design. Flowing with movement, the former deep-toned counters are replaced with a white river granite countertop paired with a timeless grey and white marble basketweave backsplash. By changing the undermount sink to a porcelain apron-style farmhouse sink, it creates balance between the apron-front range and the furniture-style cabinetry.
Photographs by Michael Hunter
Interiors by Dee Frazier Interiors, Plano, TX, page 385

BELOW: This home underwent such a renovation that Fred Nordahl Construction, Inc. took the entire roof off, and Alexander Design Group designed an entire second story add-on. This meant that I got to start the modern farmhouse kitchen entirely from scratch, so I put in black-trimmed windows to really make the white materials pop and show off the lake views. A built-in breakfast banquette, Cambria countertops, custom inset cabinetry, and high-end appliances are supported by a butler's pantry and three-season attached porch. The nickel gap ceiling and four-inch white oak flooring recede to let the handmade mosaic backsplash in Carrara and Calacatta marble shine.
Photographs by Alyssa Lee Photography
Interiors by M Gilbertson Design, Eden Prairie, MN, page 390

ABOVE TOP: Blue was the color of the day throughout this new-construction home. We wanted to create a feeling of steadiness and strength balanced by the unexpected pop of mixed colors to reflect the personality of the client. The linear and geometric patterns offered a way to keep the space feeling alive without being overwhelming.

ABOVE BOTTOM: After 30-plus years of brown, this client was looking for a decidedly white kitchen. We made it a little more special using warming tones to contrast the brightness of the chrome lighting. This unique touch offers a sophisticated flair without the space feeling cold, and was completed when we repeated the concept in the skylights.

Photographs by Plush Image Corporation

Interiors by Trust the Vision Decor, Philadelphia, PA, page 392

BELOW TOP: We were employed for the overall concept and construction of this lakeside new build, where the homeowners wanted the design to be classic and timeless. In a nod to the beautiful exterior surroundings, we specified fresh white cabinetry and a subway tile backsplash to allow the greenery to pop. The home's personality shines in the brass handles and island pendants and crisp navy island.

BELOW BOTTOM: While this home's design is predominantly traditional, the owners have a beautiful and eclectic art collection and a bent toward unusual and special pieces. This recently completed kitchen was a full gut remodel in a 30-year-old home. We incorporated a solid walnut wood top on the island and sculptural lighting to be a focal point of the space, along with full Cambria quartz backsplashes. As avid wine collectors, the owners placed an empty wine bottle inside the wall during the renovation with a note to whomever may find it in the future.
Photographs by Sqft Nashville, Emily Green

Interiors by Superior Construction and Design, Lebanon, TN, page 391

ABOVE & BOTTOM LEFT: This vibrant kitchen once sported too much of a country feel, so it was refreshed while leaving traditional accents like the ceiling beams. A high-gloss backsplash plays off the new lighting, which includes a Gregorious Pineo modern chandelier and lighted glass-front display cabinets. To the left of the doorway is the kitchen's crown jewel: a TopBrewer system that serves practically any drink imaginable thanks to its own refrigeration and plumbing line. The beautiful Ella countertop by Cambria is the finishing touch to this exquisite kitchen. The adjoining pantry features a grasscloth ceiling and Vaughn lighting fixture, drawers instead of open shelving, and LED-lighted glass cabinets on top; all behind a custom welded set of glass and iron doors. This room was honored with the top National Award Design by IDS.

BOTTOM RIGHT: Eager to recreate the Old World kitchens she knew and loved from visiting Italy, the client requested her own version of a Tuscan kitchen. The existing cabinets were kept, but painted in soft green with an antique finish, and black matte countertops were added. Bringing in a walnut-topped island provides even more seating. Statement elements such as the brickwork around the doorways, new ceiling beams, terra cotta floor tiles, and a custom range hood help the kitchen feel authentic.
Photographs by Bill Diers
Interiors by Kamarron Design, Inc, Minneapolis, MN, page 387

Interiors by Kamarron Design, Inc., Minneapolis, MN, page 387   Photograph by Mike McCaw, Spacecrafting

ML Interiors Group, Dallas, TX, page 389

Dining Spaces

Dining rooms have a reputation as the gathering space for big holiday meals and dinner parties—but why limit the room to so few occasions? They are also ideal for family game night, wine night with the girls, or formal tea time. Dining rooms have the ability to make any get-together feel special because it's not a room that you use every day. When my team and I design a dining room for homeowners, we think of these possibilities and consider the specific ways they will use and enjoy the space. And, of course, the room must be able to seat eight or more people comfortably with a table and chairs that are conducive to lingering conversations.

A few distinct elements can give a dining room personality—keeping in mind that the days of overly coordinated spaces are gone. Consider a singular dramatic element: chandelier, statement wallpaper, interesting table linens, unique chairs, mismatched tableware, or creative napkin rings. Eclectic centerpieces can be left on the table year-round, or you can add seasonal fresh flowers to keep the room inviting and bright. Accent chairs in eye-catching colors can also add character to the space.

Lighting can make or break your dining room, so don't overlook this feature if you're remodeling or designing yours. Dimmer switches are a must, and if your chandelier doesn't provide adequate light, consider adding sconces, lamps on the credenza, or recessed lighting. The mood is set with your level of light, and your dining room activities will range from bright and lively to low and relaxing. Let the space set the stage.

Michelle Lynne
ML Interiors Group, Dallas, TX

see page 389

LGB Interiors, Columbia, SC, page 389

Pamela Hope Designs, Houston, TX, page 390

Ami Austin Interior Design, Memphis, TN, page 382

ABOVE TOP: To achieve an updated look with a nod to slightly traditional but glamorous interiors, we repurposed a cherrywood table, painted it high-gloss black, and added crushed velvet chairs in a fiber-sealed finish. We also chose a clear-glass chandelier and custom curtains to pair against the classic lines in the space. The side credenza adds practical, non-bulky storage.
Photograph by Michael Hunter

ABOVE BOTTOM: With an intentional lean, the art in the dining room adds visual interest, while the sideboard offers storage for entertaining. From this angle, you can see the sitting area that was originally the less-spacious formal dining area.
Photograph by Matti Gresham Photography

FACING PAGE: We took this builder's home from spec to spectacular with a complete renovation of the kitchen. The rift-cut white oak cabinetry lends a contemporary vibe to the home's Mediterranean style. Low-profile chairs maximize sight lines from the kitchen to the living room, as well as through the doors to the gorgeous pool area. Pendants are suspended from the 22-foot ceiling and add beautiful interest without overwhelming the space.
Photograph by Emery Davis Photography

Interiors by ML Interiors Group, Dallas, TX , page 389

RIGHT & BELOW: There is a sense of scale, proportion, and balance in all of our projects, including in this dining room and bar. We incorporated the owner's favorite color—green—in various shades throughout the design, along with whites and creams. The textured rug, wallpaper, and window treatments all feature green hues. The maple bar cabinetry is Wood-Mode vista door style in a matte eclipse stain that allows the natural wood grain to show through, revealing a warm, organic pattern. The bar counter is made of tanzanite quartzite with mesmerizing veins of green, blue, and taupe, accentuated by the black walnut floating shelf from Dassoulas Custom Woodwork.

FACING PAGE TOP: The tall cabinet in the corner of the dining room provides easily accessible pantry space. Unique in its finish and style, featuring matte eclipse stain on maple from the kitchen cabinetry, it's a great complement and anchor to the dining space. The kitchen holds the homeowner's everyday essentials, but this was an ideal spot for special occasion storage. We designed the custom table in European brown quarter-sawn oak with metal legs and edging.

FACING PAGE BOTTOM: To emphasize, display, and protect the homeowner's beautiful china she inherited from her grandmother, we designed elegant built-ins featuring Wood-Mode edgemont recessed-square door style cabinetry in matte eclipse stain on maple. The custom grilles in a scalloped-shell pattern are by Architectural Grille. The wall of cabinetry frames the entry to the kitchen and feels like it has always been there, adding a polished finish to the dining space. The antique lighting and classic wallpaper from Schumacher create a serene space the owners enjoy with family and friends.
Photographs by Robert Radifera
Interiors by Aidan Design, Silver Spring, MD, page 382

ABOVE TOP: In this modern dining room, we paired vintage white swivel wingback chairs at a traditional dining table and added the Robert Kuo serving buffet to balance the silhouettes.

BOTTOM LEFT: For a classic, formal dining room, I chose camel hair indoor-outdoor velvet for the captain's chairs and a luxe leatherette for the Christian Liagre side chairs. These tricky textiles achieve the look and feel of luxury while providing savvy stain resistance along the way—function without sacrificing elegance.

BOTTOM RIGHT: In this breakfast room, we installed a series of hand-painted, one-of-a-kind paper panels on the ceiling to allow their vibrant colors and whimsical design to lift eyes—and spirits—daily. The primarily pink silk area rug is the perfect foil to the practical pleather upholstered chairs. The Tri Boi pendant, through Ralph Pucci, lends a fresh pop to finish off this fun everyday eating area.

FACING PAGE: Hello Handsome—meet Ms. Magnificent. We married these two separate sets of one-of-a-kind dining chairs to create a match for the ages. The pure silk gold rug, designer ceiling inlay, and 1960s glass-disc Murano chandelier add touches of glamour.
Photographs by Erik Johnson
Interiors by Lori Graham Design + HOME, Washington, DC, page 389

"Successful design requires a strategic mix of seemingly opposing elements such as old with new, masculine with feminine, objects from the near with textures from afar."
—Lori Graham

ABOVE & RIGHT: A well-collected home needed a bit of coordination to mix current pieces while editing out a few things that had served their time. The homeowners are art collectors, so it was fitting to have a sense of eclecticism by introducing the Murano glass chandelier with the antique mirror. Rich and elegant rugs and window treatments brought a soft harmony to the room and, of course, I simply cannot do a design without adding fresh flowers. I believe in never underestimating the beautiful pops of color and scents they add, like the fuchsia and tangerine against the celery green and gold walls.

FACING PAGE: I love getting inspiration from collections and objects that are meaningful to my clients. Embracing their collections and finding a curated, thoughtful way to display them brings inspiration and focus to the overall design process. Grouping the collection of these fabulous wood pieces did just that. The light and airy palette chosen for the room allows the collection, made up of both new and old, to be studied without a cluttered effect. I brought in depth with a hand-blown mirror from Germany to reflect the custom chandelier—with its citrine crystals and coral bark—while adding metallic paper in the alcove gives a touch of glam to keep the room ready for sparkling dinner parties.
Photographs by Sèlavie Photography
Interiors by Ami Austin Interior Design, Memphis, TN, page 382

ABOVE: When this Southern home was purchased by a not-so-Southern couple, they wanted to honor this space with the tradition that it deserves but add their flair to it. We used a John Richards chandelier to give a rainforest-like look to the dining room, and it lends a natural quality to the entire space. The gorgeous antique rug was our inspiration for the color scheme.
Photograph by Dustin Peck

FACING PAGE TOP: Traditional in all aspects, the Orlando home features classic, elegant elements. We custom-made a 90-inch round table that suits the room beautifully, along with a marble fireplace and over-sized mirror from France.
Photograph by Dustin Peck

FACING PAGE BOTTOM: From color palettes to textures, our choices for these dining rooms have strong references to nature, resulting in soothing, warm spaces.
Bottom left photograph by Robert Clark
Bottom right photograph by Dustin Peck
Interiors by LGB Interiors, Columbia, SC, page 389

BELOW: Formal dining rooms have dropped in popularity over the years in place of comfortable, informal dining spaces, which is exactly what this family opted for. We designed the room around the geometric patterns of the light fixture. You'll find the same shapes on the mirrors behind the banquette and the jack-shaped table base. We built the freestanding banquette to add casual comfort and provide flexibility to the room.
Photograph by Jack Gardner
Interiors by Brad Ramsey Interiors, Nashville, TN, page 383

BELOW TOP: Another built-in banquette, the seating in this breakfast room is attached to the wall and includes three traditional chairs. The space has plenty of pillows and is a cozy spot for coffee and conversation. The homeowners wanted a soft, airy quality to the room so we used white cut-paper art and a white chandelier to help achieve this look.

BELOW BOTTOM: This home has a small kitchen and dining space surrounded by four sets of double doors that lead outside, which makes for ideal indoor-outdoor living. We used tribal elements, geometric lines, and woven textures to achieve the look the homeowners wanted. The Kelly Wearstler pendants over the island are agate stone and steel—simple, yet eye-catching.
Photographs by Jack Gardner
Interiors by Brad Ramsey Interiors, Nashville, TN, page 383

> "Nearly all the homeowners I work with transition from being my clients to becoming dear friends for life."
> —Ginger Atherton

ABOVE: Keeping with the home's Hollywood Regency style, the entry includes 18th-century mirrors that reflect the large Baccarat chandelier. Double ottomans balance the space by lending a soft texture to the surrounding hard surfaces and coordinate with the ottomans in the nearby living room. The lamps we chose to utilize here were too short, so I added custom-carved gilded wood and Lucite bases along with custom shades to achieve the proper height.

FACING PAGE: The formal entry leads into the essential gathering space: the dining room. Deep emerald green components catch the eye, including the silk damask fabric on the chairs and the luxurious wallcovering. The room is a curated blend of old and new, resulting in a space that is timeless, elegant, and fun. A dark chest opens to reveal shocking pink-lined drawers, and sits beneath a treasure of carefully chosen accessories. Soft pink accents are found throughout the home and convey the overall whimsy and grace of the property.
Photographs courtesy of Ginger Atherton & Associates
Interiors by Ginger Atherton & Associates, Beverly Hills, CA, page 386

FACING PAGE TOP: After a busy day of work, nothing is more relaxing than enjoying a drink at a built-in home bar. Custom picture windows flood the room in daylight, reflecting off the creamy textured wallcovering, architectural glass staircase railing, and commissioned artwork. A custom cabinet and Craftsman bar table complement the open-concept floorplan design.

FACING PAGE BOTTOM: This sophisticated and luxurious transitional dining area features a custom-made adjustable maple wood table with brass finishes, velvet upholstery treatment chairs with detailed welts in contrast colors, grasscloth wallcovering, gold chandeliers, and champagne architectural design details.

BELOW: Automated window coverings, a carved bronze linear pendant, a wool tufted rug, and antique seagull wall decor turn up the temperature of this space. Foil paper wallcovering doesn't only make a bold statement, it also adds even more sophistication to this modern, minimalistic dining room.

Photographs courtesy of GAVIN GREEN HOME DESIGN LLC

Interiors by GAVIN GREENE HOME DESIGN LLC, Studio City, CA, page 386

ABOVE TOP: The biggest challenge when designing a home with a consistent neutral color palette is finding ways to offer interest and depth. Our solution was to incorporate an abundance of texture. The grey striae glazed walls create contrast against the white trim and are the perfect backdrop for the dark walnut-stained table and server. The dining chairs, which are upholstered in a faux satin, are actually easy-to-clean vinyl—beautiful and practical.

ABOVE BOTTOM: A blue Ikat print fabric was the inspiration for this New York City apartment dining room. Our client's collection of Delft pottery coordinates perfectly with the fabrics for the window treatments and dining chairs. The combination of traditional Louis XVI chairs and antique brass chandelier with the contemporary walnut table, server, and artwork contributes to its eclectic personality.

FACING PAGE: By painting the molding a creamy white, the magnificent ceiling does not overpower the symmetrically designed dining room. The coffers, as well as the dome, are painted a tarnished gold, while the stenciled damask medallion emphasizes the stunning chandelier. Mirroring the elaborate coffered ceiling—designed by Jack Wright—the area rug was custom-designed in soft gold, repeating the Greek key pattern on the upholstered chairs.
Photographs by Peter Rymwid
Interiors by Diane Durocher Interiors, Ramsey, NJ, page 386

"A well-designed home is not only a lovely backdrop— it can positively influence how our lives are lived and enjoyed."
—Diane Durocher

ABOVE: I believe in splurging strategically, and that often includes using existing pieces but highlighting them with a real showstopper, like this Gracie wallpaper. The mirror over the fireplace used to be part of a pair in the bedroom, and the window treatments came from the clients' previous house. I usually paint ceilings blue, and this one is no exception.
Photograph by Kip Dawkins
Interiors by Kelley Proxmire, Inc., Bethesda, MD, page 388

BELOW TOP: The gold trim was already there, so we worked with it and wallpapered inside the molding. More casual finishes balance the look.
Photograph by Kip Dawkins

BELOW BOTTOM LEFT: An existing dining set was dressed up with new host and hostess chairs, while the antique accent chairs received new grey flannel upholstery. The bold red wallpaper has a glossy, almost reptilian pattern to it.
Photograph by Kip Dawkins

BELOW BOTTOM RIGHT: Now that her nine children had grown up and moved out, the mother celebrated by redoing the entire first floor. She loves color and had a china collection featuring a gorgeous coral, so we amplified that with artwork and new chairs. Neutral wallpaper, a custom table and cabinet, and existing chandelier supported the fun palette.
Photograph by Stacy Zarin Goldberg

Interiors by Kelley Proxmire, Inc., Bethesda, MD, page 388

BELOW: After purchasing the classic dining table and white slipcovered chairs, it only felt natural to accent the archway with Ralph Lauren's pinstriped wallpaper. Though the clients were unsure about the crystal chandelier at first, after they saw the sparkle they agreed it helped give the black walls depth.

FACING PAGE: I'm not a fan of things being too matchy-matchy, especially with dining room chairs. So whenever I can, I mix it up by adding a complimentary bench; I like to add that feature.
Photographs by Robin Subar
Interiors by Shannon Antipov Designs, Hinsdale, IL, page 391

"In every room that I do, I like to add an antique piece, a vintage piece, and a modern piece. I like everything to feel unique and different."
—Shannon Antipov

ABOVE: After the California wildfires, we re-built this entire home from the ground up. The dining room is open to the kitchen and living room and creates a warm atmosphere for family gatherings. We sourced the dining table and chairs from local showrooms and had the window treatments custom curated by a local workroom. My client put the dining table centerpiece together beautifully for the photoshoot by drying out artichokes and displaying them alongside natural fruits for pop of color.
Photographs by Micah Trostle, Trostle Films
Interiors by Designers i, San Diego, CA, page 385

BELOW TOP: The clean, angular design of this home provides contrast to its rugged, modern desert setting. Carved into a mountainside, the home includes natural elements that we knew would work well here. The dining table is made of reclaimed eucalyptus wood and provides a warm visual link to the central fireplace. Its location in the room brings back the tradition of being in the center of the space. Floor-to-ceiling natural stone adds another layer of warmth, both literally and figuratively.

BELOW BOTTOM: The client's vision for this home was reimagined mountain architecture. The architect captured it perfectly and I added on to that with the interiors. You'll notice an eclectic mix of architecture and interior design, creating a warm, contemporary environment set in the dramatic mountain landscape. An inverse peaked, wood-plank ceiling extends outside, over the floor-to-ceiling window wall. Stone, metal, and fire make for the ideal winter combination.
Photographs by Kurt Munger
Interiors by Celaya | Soloway Interiors, Tucson, AZ, page 384

ABOVE TOP: This beautiful dining room exemplifies transitional style. We combined hues of grey and champagne to create a sophisticated, inviting area to gather. Eye-catching mirrors and contemporary art create balance with the large windows that allow natural light to pour into the space. The dining room table combined with the unique light fixture creates a warm interior.
Photographs by Olaf Growald

ABOVE BOTTOM: I use a broad range of styles and techniques, including the design of this transitional dining room. The space captures a grandeur that comes from weaving design motifs into homes. The dining room is just as functional as it is beautiful.
Photographs by Realty Pro Shots
Interiors by Susan Semmelmann Interiors, Fort Worth, TX, page 392

BELOW TOP & BOTTOM LEFT: This once Louis XVI-designed dining room was redesigned with a nod to Ralph Lauren. New curved back chairs are upholstered in rich black velvet from Holly Hunt Great Plains and you'll notice the teal and metallic gold Schumacher draperies tasseled back with exquisite tie-backs from Samuel & Sons. The addition of antiqued mirrors on specific walls opens the room up and reflects the sparkle of the original chandeliers to which black shades were added for a modern update. The clients original one-of-a-kind antique curio complements the room, as does its unique curiosities. Preserved red rose arrangements crown the refinished table that's accented with Baccarat crystal and fine silver. This room was honored with the top National Award Design by IDS.
Photographs by Bill Diers

BOTTOM RIGHT: This dining room became a show-stopper; light-colored walls and simple GP&J Baker linen draperies accent the striking black floor-to-ceiling windows framing Minneapolis' magnficent skyline. A unique zig-zag leather by Edelman Leather adorns the host chairs, and a Clarence House striped fabric was used in combination on the side chairs, echoing the clean lines of the windows. The dining table was the client's own piece and was refinished to its original luster. A Gregorius Pineo chandelier hangs in statement above the table and is complemented with antique sconces. Formations simple moss pots lend an organic touch to the finished aesthetic.
Photograph by Mike McCaw, Spacecrafting
Interiors by Kamarron Design, Inc, Minneapolis, MN, page 387

BELOW: Aubergine tones and natural linen brighten and modernize this formally brown and army-green dining room. The deep violet-toned and silver geometric wallpaper echoes the clean, modern lines found in the buffet, table, and custom linen chairs. The natural linen window treatments allow sunlight to stream through, accentuating the subtle pattern in the silky wool hand-knotted rug. We replaced the previous solid glass upper windows with custom iron grates, and installed a modern crystal chandelier with silver toned sconces. The new lighting further dims, allowing the owner to set the mood for the perfect luncheon or dinner party.
Photographs by Michael Hunter
Interiors by Dee Frazier Interiors, Plano, TX, page 385

BELOW TOP: A traditional dining room gets its edge from the silver chairs, with the patterned drapes creating drama all the way up to the ceiling. There's no other pattern in the room, so hanging the drapes to elongate the walls draws the eye up while adding a stunning sense of movement.

BELOW BOTTOM LEFT: The spectacular light fixture, custom made by a true artisan, incorporates all the elements: crystal, gold, pewter, and a rustic charcoal tone. It's a showstopper that doesn't compete with any other piece in the room.

BELOW BOTTOM RIGHT: This awkward corner space had no definition, but building in bench seating transforms it into a dining nook that also functions beautifully as a game table. Chalkboard paint adds whimsy while also providing a matte backdrop for the truly spectacular light fixture. Lighting should always flow throughout the house, complementing the furnishings while still making a statement on its own.
Photographs by Miro Dvorscak

Interiors by B. de Vine Interiors, Houston, TX, page 383

BELOW TOP LEFT: The owners' original midcentury dining set is highlighted by the wall of windows that look out into the garden. Stained wood window casings complement the furnishings and pair well with a modern light fixture and a painting from a local art professor.

BELOW TOP RIGHT: The subtle metallic gleam in the geometric paper is the perfect backdrop for the large modern art. The soft pink in the painting contrasts with the caramel saddle leather chairs and creates just a touch of tension. A linear light fixture with chunky crystals creates a contemporary line, while the traditional Oriental rug from the owners' collection plays a quiet supporting role.

BELOW BOTTOM: Clean, uncluttered, and soothing, this dining room echoes the minimalist style found throughout the rest of the home. To show off the sleek dining set, only a neutral rug and striking light fixture were needed. A major component of this house is how it was transformed from a chopped up, awkward 1980s townhome into an open and welcoming floorplan that flows easily from room to room.
Photographs by Julie Soefer
Interiors by Pamela Hope Designs, Houston, TX, page 390

ABOVE: Clean lines and architectural accents are softened by vibrant artwork that expresses a homeowner's personality and interests, while the custom mirror reflects the ever-changing beauty of New York City's Central Park.
Photographs by Regan Wood
Interiors by Elissa Grayer Interior Design, Rye, NY, page 386

ABOVE: The pale aqua walls feature insets for glass art and nautical pieces that the homeowners had collected in their native Canada. We chose this color because the golf course on which the home sits also has a lagoon located right outside the great room.

LEFT: The husband wanted to seat eight in an octagonally shaped dining room, so I worked with a company out of Texas to create the hammered metal base and sides of the large square table. The top is a textured and waxed wood, which nicely complements the transitional Thomas Pheasant chandelier—one of my favorite chandeliers ever. The chairs are a replica of an iconic loop-back design, with Schumacher fabric seats that were inspired by the artwork we found for the wall.
Photographs by Nicholas Ferris
Interiors by Collins Interiors, Longboat Key, FL, page 384

"You should live in a space that nourishes your well-being, serenity, and creativity."
—Barbara Gardner

ABOVE: This transitional dining room in an Uptown house blends vintage and modern pieces for a romantic French result. An antique Swedish sideboard holds two 19th-century iron urns with moss balls and sits beneath a print of a historic New Orleans map. The abalone-shell chandelier is from Oly and the new construction table is made of reclaimed wood with surrounding campaign chairs from Lee Industries. Dupioni silk curtains match the color of the map, while an original bead board ceiling furthers the room's character.
Photograph by Kerri McCaffety
Interiors by Tanga Winstead Designs, New Orleans, LA, page 392

ABOVE TOP: A handmade solid table is something that will stand the test of time, while plants rooting in the vases atop it are a simple décor choice that make a statement of their own. The stacked stone you see in the distance is a wood-burning fireplace, so we knew stacks of wood would be part of the patio view. Metal décor on either side of the doors balances the wood elements, along with the mirrored clock and metal and glass light fixture. All throughout is that organic feel, making this a welcoming room where you'd want to sit for a delicious meal.
Photograph by Michael Patrick Lefebvre

ABOVE LEFT: The client had a vision when it came to the kitchen island: instead of barstools at the island, they wanted a banquette-style seat so she and her husband could dine side-by-side while overlooking their expansive ocean view. An American-made solid-maple table and a few chairs to match create a vignette that prioritizes the view.
Photograph by Lisa Bruno, 64 Degrees Photography

ABOVE RIGHT: An antique table purchased in Newport, Rhode Island, and refinished became the most sought-after seat in the house. With light and sun streaming in and a view of the flower gardens and bird feeder, the effect is like being at a bed-and-breakfast every day.
Photograph by Michael Patrick Lefebvre

Interiors by Balanced Interiors, Narragansett, RI, page 383

BELOW: Living in the tranquil meadows of Michigan, peppered with Eastern white pines, the client wanted to embrace the environment they live in. The farmhouse white oak table was locally made and decorated by Jessica Crosby with buffalo check linens to inspire feelings of celebration and welcoming. The porcelain backsplash embodies Old World charm. No detail was missed—even the bread tray is made from reclaimed wood from an old schoolhouse in Bangor, Michigan.
Photographs by Troy Vanlangen, Above the Horizon Media
Interiors by Delight in Designs, Grand Rapids, MI, page 385

ABOVE LEFT: We chose sculptural Panton chairs to make a bold statement, but they're also a practical choice for a lake house (and vacation rental). The tall sloped ceiling led us to select this funky multi-level light fixture. The Barrel o' Monkeys piece by Dallas artist Michael Shellis set the playful tone and vibrant color palette for the rest of the home.

ABOVE RIGHT: This oversized piece of art commissioned from Michael Shellis deserves to be the focus of this dining space. Architecturally, we have that fantastic floating staircase and warm tongue-and-groove ceiling. We chose a black Danish modern dining table and classic Eames chairs, again for that pop of complementary color but also for easy care at the lake.

Photographs by Danny Batista

Interiors by Abode Interior Design, San Antonio, TX, page 382

BELOW: I chose a dominant color palette for this dining room, infusing purple, orange, black, and white. The combination creates a distinction against the wall's copper paint, which features acanthus leaves in wheatgrass. The bold orange area rug, with hints of yellow and splashes of white, brings a cohesiveness to the space. Strong black elements add weight and balance. You'll notice glamorous spiked gold lamps that grab the eye, along with dented gold vases and the large acanthus table base. Layered window coverings include copper, orange, and black fabrics.
Photographs by Apollo's Bow Photography

Interiors by KCL-IDESIGN, LLC, Mauldin, SC, page 388

Susan Semmelmann Interiors, Fort Worth, TX, page 392

Bedrooms

There is, perhaps, no more intimate, private space in a home than the bedroom, which means those rooms deserve that extra consideration when being designed. A master bedroom is a chance to create a retreat and a space for the homeowners to feel completely relaxed. It should meet all of their wishes, visually and functionally, and that is what I strive for with each project.

Because of my experience with homebuilding, I offer clients something unique in interior design: construction detailing. It gives my team and me the freedom to take a comprehensive approach to the space and allows us to orchestrate every aspect of the project, so bedrooms are taken to the next level. A greater amount of control in the beginning allows for a more complete design in the end—nothing is overlooked. These spaces become more personalized and suited to the homeowner's lifestyle, with an end result that's as cohesive as it is beautiful. As I always say, "the spirit of living is in the giving" and this step allows me to give more intentionally.

We also manufacture custom bedding and draperies, and carry gorgeous vendor lines of furniture, lamps, art, floral, rugs, and fabrics, giving us—and our clients—an endless amount of distinctive possibilities for the bedroom. No aspect of the room is untouched, and with the guidance and preferences of the homeowner, we can tailor all the details to make the bedroom exactly how they envision it to be.

As you look through the stunning bedrooms on these pages, notice the little things, and see how they make each unique design come alive with elegance and individual style.

Enjoy!

Susan Semmelmann
Susan Semmelmann Interiors
Fort Worth, TX
see page 392

Total 360 Interiors, Dallas, TX, page 392

Kamarron Design, Inc., Minneapolis, MN, page 387

Southern Studio Interior Design, Cary, NC, page 391

ABOVE: For a lake estate in Possum Kingdom, we opted for luxurious custom bedding, drapery, and finishes that matched the regal quality of the home. Stunning windows with ample natural light and rich antique wood pieces create a romantic and sophisticated place to rest.

PREVIOUS PAGE: We built this lake estate with Italian inspiration. The custom features of the guest bedroom play into the home's European theme with hues of aqua greens and blues, mixed with coppers and creams. The colors give the home a rustic, warm feel while the clean lines paired with ornate details make it distinct.
Photographs by Realty Pro Shots
Interiors by Susan Semmelmann Interiors, Fort Worth, TX, page 392

BELOW TOP: The master suite of this ranch home is an oasis all its own. With an expansive footprint, the room includes a state-of-the-art exercise room, an elegant bathroom, and a cozy seating area situated around a fireplace with a stunning custom mantel. We utilized soft greys and deep blues paired with fully customized bedding, window treatments, and furnishings to create the calming ambience.

BELOW BOTTOM: We were thrilled to be a part of Oxford Dream Homes, a high-end community located just north of Dallas and Fort Worth. My elegant, innovative aesthetic melded beautifully with the work of the homebuilders in this highly anticipated neighborhood featured in Fort Worth Magazine's Dream Street Homes.
Photographs by Realty Pro Shots
Interiors by Susan Semmelmann Interiors, Fort Worth, TX, page 392

"Lighting is not just illumination—it's an accessory, like jewelry."
—Elissa Grayer

BELOW & FACING PAGE: Renovating a storied 1920s Tudor estate was the ideal opportunity to show off the use of soothing color, rich texture, and layered details.
Photographs by John Bessler
Interiors by Elissa Grayer Interior Design, Rye, NY, page 386

ABOVE TOP: We designed this soft Bohemian-inspired bedroom in neutrals with a calming background. It contains layer upon layer of texture in order to ensure the color palette does not appear boring or unfinished. There is a nod to the glamour of this boudoir with the Lucite and gold drapery hardware and yards of creamy fabric.

ABOVE BOTTOM: We went with the idea of "a hotel you never have to check out of" for this bedroom. The monochromatic color palette provides a calming, elegant escape. The mirrors behind the lighting offer a functional reflection while also creating an interesting design element with the oversized nightstands, repurposed from side tables. The only thing missing is room service.
Photographs by Emery Davis Photography
Interiors by ML Interiors Group, Dallas, TX , page 389

BELOW TOP: The custom barn door was a solution to an unusual multiple-door problem in this master suite. We added shiplap for depth, texture, and to draw attention to the soaring 14-foot wall. Simple window coverings allow the eye to go toward the organic, woven material and the cozy bed linens and pillows, not to mention the striking oversized chandelier with burnished brass.
Photograph by Matti Gresham Photography

BELOW BOTTOM: In order to play on the unique window lighting in this bedroom, we kept the treatments simple—just a layer of window film to filter the light. We didn't want to darken the room so we used the unique window placement to feature the natural lighting angles. The space had a bump-out from the fireplace on the first floor's chimney leading to the exterior of the house, so we placed the bed on that wall and created custom cabinets on either side to fill the spaces. At the foot of the bed, the bench serves a practical purpose along with a nearby seating area. Soothing colors tie it all together, particularly in the art and rug.
Photograph by Stratton Creative
Interiors by ML Interiors Group, Dallas, TX , page 389

ABOVE: The square footage of this owner's bedroom created an uncommon challenge: How to create an intimate, cozy bedroom within a veritable ballroom of a space. We met the challenge head on by using wider, floor-to-ceiling drapery; a large-scale flocked wall covering with a larger-scale pattern repeat; space designating, hand-woven area rugs; and statement ceiling fixtures. The result was a bold yet elegant aesthetic that provided three inviting spaces: a sleeping area, a lounging area for movie nights, and a reflecting area for reading or meditating fireside.
Photograph by Erik Johnson

Interiors by Lori Graham Design + HOME, Washington, DC, page 389

BELOW TOP & BOTTOM LEFT: Occasionally, specific life events will drive design decisions, such as this bedroom for a recently divorced woman who reveled in the freedom of unilateral decision-making that single life affords. She wanted an unapologetically pretty-in-pink space all her own. We relied on the iconic Dorothy Draper case pieces to provide necessary touches of masculinity and modernity to balance the feminine color and patterns at play in the paint, rug, and textiles.
Photograph by Abby Greenawalt

BELOW BOTTOM RIGHT: Sometimes the unseen has the greatest impact. For these avid readers, I used the unconventional approach of running the windows to the floor in order to create the perfect nook for the bed. The bed nook is discretely flanked by hidden shelves between the primary papered wall and the set-back window wall. Stacks of books, piles of magazines and accompanying notes, reading glasses, and more live on the shelves, well within reach yet neatly hidden from view until homeowners are settled in and ready to read.
Photograph by Erik Johnson

Interiors by Lori Graham Design + HOME, Washington, DC, page 389

ABOVE: When a New York City post-grad wanted to update her childhood bedroom with Old Hollywood inspiration, the space became full of black and white glamour with strategic pops of color and lots of polished finishes. Lucite furniture accents keep the space airy and balance the glossy black lacquered and polished metal pieces. Old cabinetry was replaced with a luxe uniquely two-tone velvet sofa, creating a sitting room for relaxing and entertaining friends. Bold art bring the final statement of interest and fun to the room.

FACING PAGE TOP: As part of a master suite renovation, the space was reimagined to give the bedroom and sitting areas the view to the lake. Classic tones of grey and white simplify this master bedroom, while warm wood tones amplify the space. The space is accented with tones of charcoal and black, and adorned with curated, unique accessories. The marble feel of the wallpaper pays homage to the adjacent bathroom countertops and is aesthetically pleasing in the space. A cozy niche covered in scrumptious fabrics offers a place to decompress and relax at the end of the day. The art is part of the homeowners' private collection. This room was honored with the top National Award Design by IDS.

FACING PAGE BOTTOM: Designed to be a home away from home, this guest suite is inviting with a suite-style layout. Neutral tones envelop the space and are accented with bold black fabrics and fun accents. A cozy sitting room was designed with a sectional upholstered in luxury Romo fabric, a leather ottoman by Arteriors, and custom art from the Netherlands to add flair. Room-darkening Schumacher drapery panels are ready when needed, but the owners rarely want to shut out this view of the lake.
Photographs by Bill Diers

Interiors by Kamarron Design, Inc, Minneapolis, MN, page 387

"As a designer, I get so much joy out of hearing how much better my client's day-to-day life is in their new space."
—Kara A. Bigos

ABOVE & FACING PAGE TOP: I dubbed this master bedroom the "glam room" and it lives up to its name. Grand and chic, the space features a black king-size bed with polished nickel fittings and a large sofa in front of the bay window. Mirrors flank the bed to add depth while a custom rug features understated black, turquoise, and grey for an elegant touch.
Photograph by Jane Beiles Photography

FACING PAGE BELOW: Creams and taupes blend with traditional and primitive elements to make this master bedroom a calming space. The neutral-colored textured art piece above the fireplace is a pierced weave on linen and catches your eye immediately.
Photographs by Dustin Peck Photography
Interiors by Design Lines Signature, Raliegh, NC, page 385

"I don't take one specific approach with my work. My role is to serve as a curator and implementer of a homeowner's style, and their spaces reflect that."
—Judy Pickett

BELOW & FACING PAGE: This romantically refreshing bedroom is a place for calm reflection, with our custom signature mix of silver and pewter being the dominant color. I love the juxtaposition of mixed antique pieces with modern style, like the warm and elegant window treatments with the sleek, simple framed intaglios against the crystal chandelier, which one of our buyers spotted abroad.
Photographs by Sèlavie Photography
Interiors by Ami Austin Interior Design, Memphis, TN, page 382

231

ABOVE: The master bedroom of this Beaufort home allows for natural light to illuminate the subtle colors, making the room feel a part of the scenery. A mix of textures and soft cotton blues give the room a sky-like quality that suits the home.

FACING PAGE TOP: Our client wanted to create a guest bedroom that made visitors feel welcome, so we used traditional elements that reflect Southern hospitality. The respite offers a comfortable place to work and relax. Made from coconut shells, the Made Goods chandelier gives the room a warm glow.

FACING PAGE BELOW: Located in Columbia, South Carolina, this house captures the beauty of its lake site. The windows face the water for unobstructed views as far as the eye can see. Because the owner is a lover of French antiques, we pulled in pieces that reveal her passion without making the room overly formal.
Photographs by Robert Clark
Interiors by LGB Interiors, Columbia, SC, page 389

"My designs are as much about the site as they are the homeowners. The spaces have to make sense in their natural surroundings."
—Linda Burnside

"It's important to reserve part of your design budget for art. A room isn't complete without it."
— Brent Willmott

BELOW TOP: Simple, meaningful pieces make a room appealing. A custom bed and monogrammed bedding from Mitchell Gold + Bob Williams with a re-covered coordinating leather bench and original Andy Warhol works all come together to give this bedroom an understated sophistication.
Photograph by Jill Woodruff

BELOW BOTTOM: A little girl's dream come true, the bedroom was created as a special place for a 5-year-old with her favorite colors: soft purple and vibrant green.
Photograph by Matti Gresham

FACING PAGE: The jumping-off point for this master bedroom was the dynamic Christopher Martin painting. You can see its inspiration in the color selection and clean lines throughout the room. We used earth elements such as the petrified wood stools and natural greenery to give the contemporary space warmth.
Photograph by Matti Gresham
Interiors by Total 360 Interiors, Dallas, TX, page 392

RIGHT, BELOW & FACING PAGE: In this custom-built home with modern Tudor construction, the client requested the maximum amount of natural lighting possible. The windows take center stage, while the rest of the interior—including the master and guest bedrooms—is a blend of existing family heirlooms and new products that create a cohesive design solution that works with the soft color palette of the home.
Photographs by Lissa Gotwalls
Interiors by Bartone Interiors, Chapel Hill, NC , page 383

ABOVE TOP: The wrought iron bed, piled high with lush fabrics and pillows, is the focal point of this tranquil master bedroom. The neutral palette of light sand and pale blue is repeated throughout the space. Flanked by two built-in armoires, the stately window offers views of the spectacular property. The combination of natural beauty with the sumptuous furniture, fabric, and accessories reflects the owner's Old World Tuscan sensibilities.

ABOVE BOTTOM: The stately, king-size half-tester bed commands the master bedroom. A subtle balance of femininity and masculinity was created. The rich brocade floral and other lush fabrics offset the darker woods of the bedside tables, dresser, and armoire. The room's warmth is complemented by the pale blue of the tray ceiling and accented with creamy white trim.
Photographs by Peter Rymwid
Interiors by Diane Durocher Interiors, Ramsey, NJ, page 386

BELOW TOP: "Pretty in Pink" was the name given to our Designer Showhouse space to honor Breast Cancer Awareness Month. The soft grey modern damask wallcovering was the perfect backdrop for the pink upholstered bed. The spectacular contemporary artwork is flanked by drapery panels in a whimsical pattern. Girly and luxurious with vintage-inspired furniture, this room was a stand-out on the Showhouse tour.

BELOW BOTTOM: The Tudor-style home, which was built in the early 1900s, was the venue for many opulent events, including the homeowner's silver anniversary, four weddings, and two silent movies. The master bedroom was designed with traditional furniture pieces respectful of the home's era, but refreshed with a sophisticated palette of charcoal and cream. Incorporating lacquer, mirror accents, and contemporary artwork gives this room a more modern look. The chandelier, crystal table lamps, and accessories lend a sophisticated ambience that's reminiscent of old Hollywood glam.
Photographs by Peter Rymwid
Interiors by Diane Durocher Interiors, Ramsey, NJ, page 386

ABOVE: For a glamorous bedroom suite, I chose the finest linens and coverings without sacrificing practicality. I maximized bedside space by creating custom 26-inch nightstands. Oversized sconces add European elegance and romance to the room, while the 18th-century antique chair serves as the ideal accent.

FACING PAGE: The room's lift-top mirrored vanity has custom compartments that allow it to serve as a personal and communal space. Cosmetics, a curling iron, and other toiletries tuck away easily for a tidy, elegant look. Two 19th-century marble lamps boast hand-painted shades that I designed. A glimmering gold thread runs through the grass-cloth wallcovering, adding a touch of glamour.
Photographs courtesy of Ginger Atherton & Associates
Interiors by Ginger Atherton & Associates, Beverly Hills, CA, page 386

"If it's not going to be your best, let someone else make a mess of it"
— Ginger Atherton

ABOVE TOP: For a romantic master suite, we embellished with a custom light box, fireplace, and intimate furnishings that suit the space.

ABOVE BOTTOM LEFT: We designed a youth's bedroom to creatively address the clients' desired dual purpose. The resulting space provides a custom bunk room for children while doubling as an entertainment lounge for guests.

ABOVE BOTTOM RIGHT: A soothing bedroom exemplifies relaxed tranquility, with subtle organic drama provided by a floating teak-root sculpture.
Photographs by Mike Duerinck
Interiors by Esther Boivin Interiors, Scottsdale, AZ, page 386

BELOW TOP: An end-grain cut oak floor references the flooring that was typically used in warehouses during the turn of the 20th century. A steel-and-glass bedside table and industrial-esque floor lamps balance out the client's antique furniture. The Phillip Jeffries wool wallpaper is so cozy for a bedroom.
Photograph by Gene Meadows

BELOW BOTTOM LEFT: This primary suite features a bed custom-designed with an Edelman leather shagreen upholstered headboard with buttons down the side. The bespoke wall-mounted, rift-cut oak bedside table has a glass top that's patterned underneath to imitate the headboard's shagreen texture, adding depth and beauty.
Photograph by Stacy Zarin Goldberg

BELOW BOTTOM RIGHT: The homeowners wanted something simple and chic that ultimately felt comfortable and livable. The NYC blanket is a keepsake from their travels, while the artwork is the homeowner's own photography. A classic Nelson Platform bench completes the look at the foot of the bed.
Photograph by Stacy Zarin Goldberg
Interiors by Design Milieu, Washington, DC, page 385

ABOVE TOP: Where else but in the Bahamas would a suspended bed be a natural solution? There's a nautical feeling with the ropes, but the tranquil teal and cheerful coral also nod to the Baker's Bay location. As a guest room, it creates the perfect vacation fantasy.

ABOVE BOTTOM: The design of this master bedroom in the same Bahamas home had to complement, and not overtake, the stunning views of the ocean. A custom walnut bed was among the furnishings and soft goods made in South Florida and then shipped over, meaning that careful planning was even more vital.
Photographs by Kim Sargent
Interiors by Chad Renfro Design, Palm Beach, FL, page 384

BELOW: This bedroom created a challenge that we used to the homeowners' advantage. Behind the screen is an odd doorway to storage, and it was the only wall large enough for the king-size bed. Custom folding screens were created to flank the bed, hiding the door. The soft backdrop added a cool design element behind the bedside tables and emphasized the slope in the ceiling.
Photograph by Dustin Peck
Interiors by Knight Carr & Company, Greensboro, NC, page 388

ABOVE: In a complete master suite remodel, the original space combined two strangely angled teal and burgundy rooms that had been filled with awkward moldings and a less than desirable use of space. The bedroom sitting area and main area were previously divided by a brass fireplace. While the bedroom floorplan had an abundance of space, the bathroom lacked functionality. With a love of color, the couple desired a room filled with artistic modern colors in a spa-like oasis. With a starting point of a showstopping bold abstract rug, we selected spainspired teals mixed with romantic furnishings. Custom teal swivel chairs allow the couple to sit and turn to enjoy the garden out the window. Using new decorative trims and moldings, the tray cover ceiling's ambient lighting is concealed. Mirrors are placed throughout in various forms and functions in both the master suite and bathroom, allowing natural light to reflect into and around the space. The sheer window panels allow the couple privacy without blocking the picturesque garden view.

Photographs by Michael Hunter
Interiors by Dee Frazier Interiors, Plano, TX, page 385

BELOW The high-end finishes and collected art in this Central Park West apartment are tempered with a healthy dose of comfort, humor, and practicality.
Photographs by Regan Wood
Interiors by Elissa Grayer Interior Design, Rye, NY, page 386

BELOW TOP: This bachelor's master bedroom's statement piece is the 3-D, MDC metallic wallcovering. The bed is flanked by Restoration Hardware metal-wrapped nightstands to add to the modern industrial feel. We softened the look with an oversized tufted headboard and two custom wooden globe light fixtures.
Photograph by Leslee Mitchell

BELOW BOTTOM: Our goal in designing this master bedroom, located in a historic four-square in downtown Nashville, was to blend contemporary with traditional, old with new. The dark bronze metal canopy bed with a custom leather headboard brings the new, the historic brick and reclaimed wood feature wall bring the old. The dresser combines natural wood elements on the front drawers with a contemporary lacquered finish on the top and sides.
Photograph by Reagen Taylor
Interiors by JL Design, Nashville, TN, page 387

ABOVE TOP: To help create a calm, relaxed space for a master bedroom, we draped the wall behind the bed and chose a monochromatic color scheme with varied textures. The tree-print design on the window treatments were tinted to match the patterned sheers and add visual appeal to the quiet space.

ABOVE BOTTOM: Walnut features repeat throughout this home, including the master bedroom's accent wall. The room has many points of interest, including the basket-weave leather headboard, floating-wood nightstands, and wall-mounted lamps. You'll notice the Airedale terrier statue as a nod to the homeowner's and designer's love of the breed.
Photographs by Steve Bracci Photography
Interiors by Laurie McRae Interiors, Augusta, GA, page 388

ABOVE: A narrow entrance to the master suite adds to the drama of the room's 14-foot ceilings, while the neutral palette is set off by subtle details with big impact. The fireplace has an eye-catching reflective plaster finish and the two pieces of art on the wall are made with porcupine quills—both of which add texture and interest to the space. You'll also notice woven African baskets and custom-curated patterns on the bed.
Photographs by Jack Gardner
Interiors by Brad Ramsey Interiors, Nashville, TN, page 383

BELOW: The entire home exudes a warmth thanks to the depth of materials, and the master retreat is no exception. The bedroom offers a sitting area where the couple can enjoy a movie, relax by the fire, or take in the West Coast views. Meant to be a soothing escape, the bedroom is a place to let stress melt away.
Architect: Daniel Fletcher / Architects PC
Photographs by Aaron Leitz Photography
Interiors by Carson Guest, Atlanta, GA, page 384

BELOW TOP: Floral wallpaper on the headboard wall sets the tone for this master bedroom. The bed itself is upholstered in a faux ostrich skin with a grey wood-toned frame. The light silk bedding creates a cozy place to relax. I found a hand-painted silverleaf cabinet to anchor the TV area. Just beyond the master bedroom is a sitting room with two comfortable chairs and a luxurious desk area, which serves as the lady of the house's sanctuary.

BELOW BOTTOM: The headboard wall features an elegant swirl designed with tone-on-tone wallpaper and glass beads. The crystal chandelier and lamps accent the mirror-front nightstands, while the upholstered bed in an aqua fabric coordinates with the beautiful custom bedding. We also wanted to add a comfortable sitting area where you can just read a book and glance outside at the beautiful Gulf of Mexico.
Photographs by Sam Arnold, HomeAndDesignPhotography.com
Interiors by Aniko Designs, Fort Myers, FL, page 382

ABOVE TOP: This expansive master bedroom offered a coastal vibe with its steel blues and weathered woods. The clients wanted a relaxing sanctuary that beckoned to her youth on the farm and his days spent on the water.

ABOVE BOTTOM: Handmade porcelain flowers, along with a soothing lavender color, anchored this feminine hideaway. A place all her own to get away from it all was not only what she wanted, but needed. This space was our offering.
Photographs by Plush Image Corporation
Interiors by Trust the Vision Decor, Philadelphia, PA, page 392

ABOVE: At this award-winning luxury vacation rental property on the shores of Lake LBJ, the objective was to be bold, colorful, and fun. Each room was designed to be memorable, making it hard to choose where to rest your head after a day spent on the water. The Palm Room features an eye-catching accent wall papered with Schumacher's Zebra Palm design, while the accent wall in the Frida Room is painted a bold black to make the original art really pop. The Bunk Room needed to appeal to all ages and genders, so we used three aquatic-inspired colors to create a graphic wall design.
Photographs by Danny Batista
Interiors by Abode Interior Design, San Antonio, TX, page 382

BELOW TOP: A well-known Schumacher fabric became a throw that the wife uses on chilly nights; there is also an extra cashmere blanket on the chaise in her reading corner. The husband, meanwhile, has a comfy swivel chair if they'd like to chat. Pieces such as the stunning Circa lamps and mirror encircled in real porcupine quills make a statement without disrupting the bedroom's tranquility.

BELOW BOTTOM: This guest bedroom is a private, comfy space with its own balcony overlooking the water, and comes in handy as a sroom for their new grandchild and parents. The bedside chests are made of faux shagreen with fun tassels as the pulls, a pattern that is subtly echoed by the fish motif on the ceramic lamps. The shapely headboard is custom made by OOMPH, and there is a daybed on the other side of the room for when the grandchild is a little older.
Photographs by Nicholas Ferris

Interiors by Collins Interiors, Longboat Key, FL, page 384

TOP LEFT: The reclaimed ceiling beams and soft greige on the walls and ceiling touch on Mediterranean influences. Soft velvet bedding and embroidered drapery soften this master bedroom, which has access to a beautiful pool and inviting veranda.
Photograph by Julie Soefer

TOP RIGHT: A large abstract piece of art draws in colors found throughout the room and brings your eye up to the pitched ceiling and edgy metal light fixture.
Photographs by Colleen Duffley

BOTTOM LEFT: Sand-colored sisal and sage-colored fabrics were used throughout this second master suite, with a surprise ceiling covering in a small geometric paper.
Photographs by Colleen Duffley

BOTTOM RIGHT: A cheerful metallic butterfly wallcovering from Thibaut creates a cheerful backdrop for the silverleaf end tables and whimsical mirror. A play on pattern unfolds with the animal-print drapery and lattice rug. The velvet-covered bed welcomes any guest to come and soak in the views of the bay and natural wildlife.
Photographs by Colleen Duffley

Interiors by Melanie King Designs, The Woodlands, TX, page 389

BELOW TOP: Everything in this master bedroom is customized: the large-format porcelain-tile fireplace, motorized Roman shades that tie into the ensuite color and accented by an Oly table, Cisco Brothers slip-covered swivel chairs, and custom oak flooring. Because the homeowners have an elderly dog, we used an outdoor fabric in a snakeskin print for the custom bedding that makes clean-up a breeze.

BELOW BOTTOM: Feminine, romantic, and transitional, this master bedroom is a relaxing escape. To create a warm, retreat-like setting, I chose taupe and blush tones, Dupioni silk curtains, a mirrored pickled-oak armoire, and a beckoning metallic chaise lounge. The Carrerra fireplace surround and art from Ida Floreak add to the elegance of the room.
Photographs by Kerri McCaffety
Interiors by Tanga Winstead Designs, New Orleans, LA, page 392

TOP LEFT: We were thrilled to contribute our design flair to this elegant retreat that was architecturally designed by Norris Architecture. This space became all about finishes, textures, and patterns to create a soft, rich, and welcoming dream bedroom.
Photograph by Stacy Zarin Goldberg

TOP RIGHT: By incorporating layers of beautiful Stroheim fabrics for the drapes that showcase the marble-top nightstand, it complements the other layered textures on the bed to create interest, softness, and design harmony.
Photograph by Stacy Zarin Goldberg

BOTTOM LEFT: This transitional bedroom is rich in texture, with a soft color palette accented with metallic custom drapes. We added a little glam to this bedroom with fabrics, colors, and textures that come together to draw you in and make a sophisticated statement.
Photograph by Christy Kosnic
Interiors by GreyHunt Interiors, Chantilly, VA, page 387

BELOW TOP: This master bedroom combines rich textures and a soft grey monochromatic palette to create a warm and relaxing space. Hydrangeas are softly captured in the wonderful Impressionistic oil painting, while the grey palette is enhanced with coordinating grey trim and wainscoting.
Photograph by INSPIRO 8 STUDIOS

BELOW BOTTOM: A wall of window treatments softly frames this dramatic master bedroom, which blends contemporary fabric with wood and metal furnishings to create an inviting space to relax in at the end of the day. Unique, hexagon-style chairs and the coordinating ottoman are perfect for curling up with coffee or a glass of wine.
Photograph by Getz Images
Interiors by Ca'Shae Interior Design, Roswell, GA, page 383

ABOVE: People often request that their master bedroom be a true retreat, so we focus on comfortable seating, soft textures, and soothing colors. Power blinds, hidden behind lush drapery, provide the final touch toward achieving total relaxation.
Photographs by Dustin Peck Photography
Interiors by Southern Studio, Cary, NC, page 391

BELOW TOP: A very brave husband decided to surprise his wife with a master bedroom remodel while she was away on a two-week business trip. After having renovated the common areas of the home, it was time they prioritized their own sanctuary. With help from their daughter, we chose her favorite hues and plenty of soft furnishings to create not just a visually appealing room, but one that allows them to rejuvenate and relax from a hectic modern life. Ultimately, his wife loved it when she returned.

BELOW BOTTOM: When adding this master suite, the inspiration came from a quaint Scottish inn in Edinburgh, Scotland, that the owners had visited and loved. French doors lead out to a lovely patio, which if you use your imagination could double as an English garden.
Photographs by Michael Patrick Lefebvre
Interiors by Balanced Interiors, Narragansett, RI, page 383

Bathrooms

Bathrooms are the most personal rooms in a home, and often where people spend time alone for much-needed moments of respite. Unlike other spaces, bathrooms aren't meant for gathering or entertaining, which makes the demands of the space unique. Here I get the opportunity to marry function and form, optimizing luxury and comfort without sacrificing any of the practical needs.

Over the years, bathrooms have increasingly taken on more of a spa-like quality. Most of my clients want a haven to escape to in the evenings and a peaceful place to prepare for the day in the mornings. Calming shades of grey, white, cream, and taupe are ideal for creating a serene bathroom, but that doesn't mean there can't be elements of surprise woven into the design. I like to use accessories with pops of color for a touch of bright, eye-catching drama.

Although guest baths and powder rooms are much smaller and don't get the same attention as master bathrooms, they have the capacity to make a big impact on visitors. It's one of the few times that guests are completely alone in a room, giving them time to study and take in details of the space. This is my chance to create something private, luxurious, and beautiful that will have an impact.

No two bathrooms—or any rooms that I design—are the same. I love trying new ideas and combinations, so each room has a singular appeal. I search for constant visual stimulation and always look to spice up my designs to keep it interesting. This approach has worked well for homeowners over the years, as the result is a timeless aesthetic that remains engaging.

Have fun,

Lori Carroll
Lori Carroll & Associates
Tucson, AZ
see page 389

Lisa Gielinki Interior Design, Jacksonville, FL, page 389

Melanie King Designs, The Woodlands, TX, page 389

Esther Boivin Interiors, Scottsdale, AZ, page 386

264　INSPIRED INTERIORS

BELOW: We used the elements of this bathroom to craft a light, modern space. The clean lines of the white wall-mounted porcelain Lacava sink stand out against the patterned Tileshop backsplash with metallic glaze. The eye-catching pendant is comprised of frosted glass with a satin nickel finish.

FACING PAGE: For a full remodel, we completely demolished the existing bathroom, and although it was a time-consuming and messy project, the end results were worth it. Whites, greys, and browns come together beautifully. The Brittanica custom vanity sinks are made of quartz and feature a ceramic Subway Lab backsplash in a gloss-white finish, with ceramic 5-by-5-inch white-matte accent tiles. The Punti stone floor has a natural cinder-grey finish.

PREVIOUS PAGE: It's hard to believe that this bathroom was originally a wine room, built into the side of a mountain. We had the room outfitted with proper plumbing, and because a main waste line was inaccessible in this remote spot, we opted for a composting toilet that doesn't require running water.
Photographs by Jon Mancuso
Interiors by Lori Carroll & Associates, Tucson, AZ, page 389

BELOW: If a homeowner insists on sticking to a strict budget, we honor that. We sourced interesting materials and finishes that were also affordable for this bathroom. The green accent tiles are semi-gloss quarter-round glazed ceramic with a citric bloom finish that pops. You'll notice that the hardware is chrome—from Klodea—which complements the white sinks and polished marble countertop. We used Diesel hard leather flooring in ivory with a natural finish to add to this on-budget aesthetic.
Photograph by Jon Mancuso
Interiors by Lori Carroll & Associates, Tucson, AZ, page 389

Photographs by Bill Lesch

ABOVE TOP LEFT: We completely transformed a bathroom that was originally outdated and cramped. A vibrant, bronze, circular mirror and distinct wall light creates interest in the small space while still being functional.

ABOVE TOP RIGHT: When we created a powder room that had to work with the space's unique radius behind the vanity, we used beveled tiles to accommodate the curve. The Bocci pendant lighting, custom metal wall panels, and slanted-slab charcoal tile make this bathroom stand out.

ABOVE BOTTOM LEFT: Our client previously owned the light fixtures used in this project. We wanted to include these rustic fixtures but still create a contemporary setting.

ABOVE BOTTOM RIGHT: When a room has a beautiful view, it makes sense to take advantage of it. We used a sliding mirror to incorporate the Tucson Mountains in the backdrop without sacrificing practical needs.

Photographs by Bill Lesch

Interiors by Lori Carroll & Associates, Tucson, AZ, page 389

BELOW: The original location of this bathroom wasted a great deal of space. It was reworked, which rewarded the master suite with a more complimentary layout for not only the bathroom, but also for the entry hall, his-and-hers closets, and bedroom. The oversized mirrors enhance the room's grandeur and reflect the natural light from the windows. Custom his-and-hers vanities are precious to the owners as well as a dedicated make-up space. Concrete subway tiles clad the walls while Cambria covers the counters. A hidden pop-up TV, show-stopping carved stone tub, open shower with a window, and modern finishes complete the look. This room was honored with the top National Award Design by IDS.

FACING PAGE TOP LEFT: This space is aesthetically unique in a brilliant way. With no shortage of craftsmanship, each individual piece of woven walnut DuChateau was carefully laid out by skilled carpenters prior to installation. The rustic stone floor is a perfect tribute to the stunning walnut vanity and massive iron mirror. The contemporary sconces, silverleaf ceiling, and *Girl On Trapeze* by Corbin Bronze assisted in modernizing this unparalleled powder room. This room was honored with the top National Award Design by IDS.
Photographs by Bill Diers
Interiors by Kamarron Design, Inc, Minneapolis, MN, page 387

ABOVE TOP RIGHT: Two separate bathrooms were created from what was once a Jack-and-Jill bathroom. Designed for twins, they wanted different designs with a unified look as they had similar tastes: modern and clean. Corner showers were designed with linear drains, clad in white stone. Storage was accommodated with corner cabinets and storage over the toilet. The floating vanity with jaw-dropping wrapped stone finishes this contemporary bathroom. This room was honored with the top National Award Design by IDS.

ABOVE BOTTOM RIGHT: The design for the powder room focused on modernism, giving the small space style and interest. Adding depth, the textured tile walls play well with the polished penny tile floor as it bounces the layered light. The unique carved-wood belted vanity adds a fun flair, and the wooden fish float on the wall as a nod to its lakeside location.

ABOVE BOTTOM LEFT: This stunning powder bathroom with its own sitting room was reimagined with elegance. We took its Louis XVI roots and added an updated brushstroke wallpaper in soft hues of green and gold accentuated by newly painted off white millwork. The sitting space was enhanced with a new silk and wool-blend rug and silk pull-apart rouched draperies framing the original chandelier. Several Lalique glass sculptures adorn the room, catching the light from the extra-tall windows. This room was honored with the top National Award Design by IDS.
Photographs by Bill Diers

Interiors by Kamarron Design, Inc, Minneapolis, MN, page 387

ABOVE: The wet area of a master bathroom shows off five-star resort features. I centered the dramatic space with back-lit blue onyx to provide a jaw-dropping aesthetic.
Photograph by Mike Duerinckx

RIGHT: Glamorous themes with bright red accents define this lady's area of the master suite.
Photograph by Mike Duerinckx

FACING PAGE TOP LEFT: We chose exciting elements to make this powder room fun. You'll notice the cubist-inspired tile design and custom vanity that offers unexpected entertainment for the eyes.
Photograph by Tony Mannella

FACING PAGE TOP RIGHT: My dramatic instincts shine in this custom master suite vanity. I incorporated indirect lighting accented with decorative light-saber chandeliers.
Photograph by Mike Duerinckx

FACING PAGE BOTTOM LEFT: Clean linear influence was the theme for this master bathroom. The mirrors reveal reflections of a clustered light sculpture.
Photograph by Mike Duerinckx

FACING PAGE BOTTOM RIGHT: I created this bathroom to serve as an escape from reality for the homeowners and their visitors. The fantasy powder room features many unexpected and creative custom features.
Photograph by Mike Duerinckx
Interiors by Esther Boivin Interiors , *Scottsdale, AZ, page 386*

"Technical skill and creativity are required in equal measure to deliver a true sense of place, function, and aesthetic."
—Lisa Gielincki

BELOW TOP: His-and-hers sides, including the entrances and controls, give the homeowners complete control of their preferences. A full wall of glass tile accents the bathtub and makes it a focal point in the room.

BELOW BOTTOM LEFT: At first glance this powder room seems entirely Old World, but then you notice the Lucite pedestal on the sink and mirrored tiles.

BELOW BOTTOM RIGHT: A sleek, contemporary master bath includes a custom vanity and mirrors, which were built out to properly hold the sconces. An extra-thick chiseled countertop edge adds heft.

FACING PAGE: One giant slab of stone along the back wall is like living art, and it's coordinated with the cabinets to not feel too overwhelming. The sunken bathtub inside the shower creates a truly indulgent wet room.
Photographs by Jessie Preza

Interiors by Lisa Gielincki Interior Design, Jacksonville, FL, page 389

ABOVE: The real star of this master bathroom is the tile selection. We sourced hand-made imported tile from Austin's own Clay Imports for the shower walls and a triple hexagon porcelain for the bathroom floor. The shower wall tiles are laid in a double herringbone pattern to contrast a large, dramatic black hexagon pattern on the bathroom floor. We accented the black tiling with two black patterned barn doors at the bathroom's entrance and closet, and created stylish, functional storage by installing custom cabinets made from naturally stained white oak. Getting rid of a large, outdated, and rarely used tub freed up so much space that we were able to expand the shower and add a large window to allow natural light to flood the space.
Photographs by Sarah Natsumi Moore
Interiors by Urbane Design, Austin, TX, page 392

BELOW: The clients' style is eclectic and fun—the more visual interest, the better. A unique challenge here was the size of the master bath; adding a laundry room, separate water closet, and enlarging the shower and vanity was a tall order. Since square footage was not on our side, we opted for white cabinets, floors, and countertops that reflect light and give the appearance of more space. Sliding barn doors made from reclaimed wood were added to the bathroom entrance and a shared door used for either the new laundry and water closet to save space, offer privacy, and add an element of surprise to the room. This is the perfect example of design that does not have to trade function for beauty—it accomplishes both seamlessly.
Photographs by Chase Daniel
Interiors by Urbane Design, Austin, TX, page 392

ABOVE: A classic grey and white palette comes alive in this Capitol Hill row home's master bedroom. The Wood-Mode colony recessed door-style cabinetry in platinum opaque finish with Calacatta gold-honed marble countertops creates a balanced space—not too warm, not too cold. Sourced from Dassoulas Custom Woodworks, the reclaimed wood-framed mirror serves as a focal point and adds depth to the room. The café milk gloss ceramic tile and Calacatta gold-honed herringbone mosaic tile let the polished nickel details shine, including the Top Knobs Ascendra pulls, Circa Lighting's Aspect sconces, and Kohler Margaux plumbing fixtures. We maximized shower space and used an oversized sink with double faucets to make the bathroom as functional as possible.

FACING PAGE: Warm and cool elements come together for a highly personalized bathroom with maple cabinets in charcoal and vanity wall tiles in powder blue clear glass. This homeowner had skin sensitivities that we took into account while designing, including incorporating aromatherapy features in the tub. We also borrowed space from a neighboring room to give her a functional shower, maximized storage with cut-out drawers, and minimized the tub deck, giving the room an overall clean, bright aesthetic. Wood elements, such as asymmetric floating shelves in walnut with matte shale stain and the teak bench inside the shower, offer a natural feel.
Photographs by Robert Radifera
Interiors by Aidan Design, Silver Spring, MD, page 382

ABOVE: The husband wanted a luxurious shower, while the wife desired a tub she could practically disappear into. They each got their wish, with a herringbone-patterned floor, floating cabinets with lights underneath, skylights above, and large-format porcelain tile that was matched so perfectly it looks like one giant piece of stone.

FACING PAGE TOP: The footprint of the master bath in this Galleria high-rise wasn't terribly large to begin with, but I managed to give the owners a double vanity, separate shower, and freestanding tub, as well as a dedicated makeup area.

FACING PAGE BOTTOM LEFT: This barrier-free bathroom, which I think of as "the gentleman's bathroom," was made accessible with a curb-less shower and a focus on lower storage.

FACING PAGE BOTTOM RIGHT: Imagine pink tile and segmented areas in this bathroom, which sits in a house built in the 1960s. By opening up the space, we made room for a shower large enough for his-and-hers sides. A cabinet piece that's typically used for wine storage here becomes the spot for extra towels, while a panel of frosted glass provides privacy around the toilet.
Photographs by Miro Dvorscak
Interiors by Chandra Stone Interior Design, Houston, TX, page 384

"Inspiration is all around us."
—Chandra Stone

ABOVE: I used a play of mirror-on-mirror to give unlimited depth to a remodeled bathroom in a Georgian-style home. Light fixtures on top of the mirrors increase reflection and dimension.

FACING PAGE: A contemporary bathroom features a his-and-hers vanity with warm walnut walls, European oak floors, and black granite. A deep backyard and motorized shades ensure privacy, as the sculptural soaking tub overlooks the garden.
Photographs by Steve Bracci Photography
Interiors by Laurie McRae Interiors, Augusta, GA, page 388

"Universal design accounts for the inherent ages and abilities in people, and make a space endlessly usable."
—Laurie McRae

BELOW & FACING PAGE TOP: The homeowner had seen my work in a spec home and sought me out to design her home, giving me free rein. I made the master bathroom's focal point the tile floor, contrasting it with the cabinetry for a soothing, serene atmosphere. A 6-by-6-foot walk-in shower even boasts a view of the trees outside.

FACING PAGE BOTTOM: This guest bathroom is where the grandkids go after their time in the pool, so my colleague Anne Elizabeth Barbe and I made a statement with the tile floor in shades of blue and white. Mixing metals with brass and polished nickel helped it feel more modern, and does the curb-less shower.
Photographs by Keith Trigaci
Interiors by Patrice Rios Interiors, Austin, TX, page 390

"The world of design is ever-changing, but spaces should always be thoughtful and timeless."
—Patrice Rios

ABOVE: The master bathroom of the Possum Kingdom estate shows off cabinetry with shades of aqua and gold. The gorgeous light fixtures lead you into the bathtub space that boasts ample amounts of natural light, creating an oasis. Italian arches meet warm lighting, and help make a relaxing and opulent Mediterranean getaway. The stunning bathroom vanity comes together with light hues of blue and rich tan colors. Careful ornamentation on the mirrors creates an exquisite focal point that draws the eye up.

FACING PAGE: This master retreat is meant to be an escape, and we kept that in mind during every decision of the process. Spa-like and serene, the suite includes an elegant bathroom with a stunning chandelier over the tub and intricate tiling throughout. Blues and greys offer a sense of calm to the space.
Photographs by Realty Pro Shots
Interiors by Susan Semmelmann Interiors, Fort Worth, TX, page 392

"*Every family has a beautiful, exceptional story, and having a home that reflects your story is priceless.*"
—Karen Hattan

BELOW & FACING PAGE: Recent transplants to Tennessee, my clients wanted to merge their classic New England aesthetic with a more laid-back Southern feel. Working with the existing neutral tile and gold fixtures, I installed a blue mosaic tile border around the tub. The simple addition packs a punch, both in modernizing the bath surround and showcasing the room's updated color palette. A soft spa-blue hue rejuvenates the vanity, while the gorgeous wallcovering by Anna French—with its subtle paisley pattern—lends a sense of sophisticated tranquility. Painting the storage towers an ivory-white minimized their visual impact, allowing the new gold mirrors and wallpaper to take center stage. Plantation shutters above the tub are a nod to the home's locale and further emphasize the classic-meets-casual look of the entire room.
Photographs by J. Totten Photo
Interiors by Home by Hattan, Nashville, TN, page 387

BELOW: Hand-selected wall panels of specialty crafted stone on paper gave us Old World charm while keeping this design looking fresh with a unique sense of style. The contemporary bronze sconces flanking the custom vessel sink further the look. We would like to think this powder room could not perfectly exist in any other home.
Photographs by Sêlavie Photography
Interiors by Ami Austin Interior Design, Memphis, TN, page 382

ABOVE TOP LEFT: A shimmering glass mosaic is the backdrop for a vanity by Neo Metro that's topped with a cast-resin countertop and a polished stainless steel bowl. The wall-mounted waterfall spout faucet is attached to a sleek shelf for more functionality, while a semi-custom piece below by Lacava adds storage.
Photograph by Stacy Zarin Goldberg

ABOVE TOP RIGHT: Lacava is also behind this zebrawood vanity with an extra-large sink. Travertine tile stops just below the lights from Steng and a mirror from BDDW.
Photograph by Stacy Zarin Goldberg

ABOVE BOTTOM: A marble tub apron and top is accented by a wide stripe of inset glass tile on both the wall and floor, which is finished with porcelain tile by Diesel Living. The custom Lacava vanity adds warmth with its wood tones.
Photograph by Gene Meadows
Interiors by Design Milieu, Washington, DC, page 385

ABOVE: With quietude and relaxation as the goal of this bathroom, softness of touch, diaphanous separations, and matte surfaces drift through the doorways. Seamless access to the private outdoor deck and views of the lake to the north find the distant opposite shore, like the interiors, bathed in light.

RIGHT: When built form reaches to embrace and enclose, especially in small spaces, scale of the human body and the experience of the moment take priority over group interactions and shared activity. These are spaces which every home needs, for individuals to rest, breathe, and purposefully withdraw into memories and dreams.
Photographs by Andrea Rugg
Interiors by CF Design Ltd, Duluth, MN, page 384

"Creativity depends on empathy and passion. Imagination introduces the opening act of creativity, and storytelling is the means by which we convey our ripening ideas. We all have these capacities."
—Cheryl Fosdick

ABOVE: There's a "wow" effect when you first enter the master bathroom—lighting is so critical to the overall impression of a space. The bathroom is basically split down the middle, with his-and-hers vanities, closets, and entries to the walk-in shower all meeting at the standalone soaking tub.
Photograph by Miro Dvorscak

Interiors by B. de Vine Interiors, Houston, TX, page 383

TOP & ABOVE RIGHT: Choosing the correct finishes and fixtures meant paying homage to the Harrison, New York, home's grand history, but also making the rooms feel fresh and modern in convenience.
Photographs by John Bessler

ABOVE LEFT: The sleekness of the high-rise's environment was balanced by warm wood tones and natural materials.
Photograph by Regan Wood
Interiors by Elissa Grayer Interior Design, Rye, NY, Page 386

ABOVE LEFT: There is a pleasing simplicity with black and white—how fresh it looks, especially in a bathroom. Hexagonal tiles were a way to incorporate a larger scale without using standard squares, and using grey grout conceals the effects of everyday living.
Photograph by Christy Kosnic

ABOVE RIGHT: Upon opening the door to this powder room you're hit with the bold and exciting Fabricut wallpaper, which packs quite a design punch. The crisp white of the mirror and pedestal sink balance out their interesting curves, while Circa lighting ties it all together. There's even a peep of green ceiling that's cohesive to the palette in the rest of the house.
Photograph by Stacy Zarin Goldberg

RIGHT: There is so much stunning texture in this Calcatta marble that we installed it halfway up the wall. An on-the-wall faucet allows the marble to be enjoyed even more fully.
Photograph by Stacy Zarin Goldberg
Interiors by GreyHunt Interiors, Chantilly, VA, page 387

ABOVE TOP LEFT: Playing further on the organic elements of the mountain terrain, this powder room blends natural materials. Notice the textures of hand-carved marble walls, the hand-scraped walnut vanity, and a natural stone sink—all highlighted by a blown-glass chandelier.

ABOVE TOP RIGHT: We used contemporary design to create an extraordinary space in a powder room featuring a combination of contrasting materials. It includes textured metal vanity legs, a marble sink, tile accent wall, and floating ceiling.

ABOVE BOTTOM: Floor-to-ceiling windows in a master bathroom offer stunning views of the mountains and saguaro cacti, yet still maintain a sense of seclusion.
Photographs by Kurt Munger
Interiors by Celaya | Soloway Interiors, Tucson, AZ, page 384

BELOW: We wanted to incorporate the husband and wife's style in this master bathroom, which meant combining contemporary and traditional elements without sacrificing the integrity of the home. The entire design is a balancing act, with warm and cool tones used throughout the space. Modern pieces include the Timothy Oulton chandelier and vivid art that feels natural against the wall. A bath mat, small table, and stool for undressing are practical touches for the lady of the house, who often takes baths. The master vanity features custom rift-cut oak cabinet fronts with "black fox" lacquer finish and the mirrors show off an inverted triangle design, mimicking the tile pattern behind the soaker tub. Outfitted with all the bells and whistles, the steam shower is lined with porcelain Daltiles and includes two shower heads, a handheld fixture, body sprays, and an under-lit bench that gives the small space a dreamy quality.
Photographs by Reagen Taylor
Interiors by JL Design, Nashville, TN, page 387

BELOW: A classic white, grey, and black palette works beautifully for an elegant, contemporary bathroom. We chose white and grey Carrara marble accent tile for niches by the tub and in the shower. A wall-mounted vanity with raised sinks fits the space perfectly. All the plumbing features have polished chrome finishes, while round mirrors and a sleek water glass and black pendant adorn the vanity for a clean aesthetic. We added contemporary art and a fabric Roman shade for color and interest. A practical accent table sits by the tub to hold items for bathing.
Photographs by Scott Johnson Photography
Interiors by KP Designs, Louisville, KY, page 388

ABOVE TOP: In the guest bathroom, we removed the bathtub to create a large frameless shower beneath the skylight. The shower walls are covered with neutral Bursa beige marble, while Emperador marble accents the storage niches and shower floor for a warm and sophisticated feeling.
Photograph by Rebecca McAlpin Photography

ABOVE BOTTOM LEFT: In this hall bathroom, touches like a honed-marble floor with a decorative border and Carrara marble wrapping the tub alcove add understated luxury. The wood-panel front echoes the dove grey vanity; these lend a softness that complements the glass-enclosed, ceramic-tile shower with its top and bottom stripes of Bardiglio marble. Custom tub and shower niches add an upscale feel.
Photograph by Rebecca McAlpin Photography

ABOVE BOTTOM RIGHT: Various sizes and shapes of Calacatta marble tile set the stage for luxury in this ensuite bathroom. The generously sized bathtub features an oversized custom niche and is surrounded on three sides by marble for a cozy soak.
Photograph by Paul S. Bartholomew Photography

Interiors by Glenna Stone Interior Design, Philadelphia, PA, page 386

ABOVE: Each and every one of the beveled mirror pieces for this jaw-dropping bathroom wall was measured and hand-cut on-site. For even more drama, we hung two Venetian mirrors over it all, and completed the look with all-custom finishes.
Photograph by Scott Smallin
Interiors by Legacy Interiors, Myrtle Beach, SC, page 388

BELOW TOP LEFT: By simplifying the original shower and tub areas, which were heavy and had little natural light, we opened up each space, lightened the palette, and pulled in unique tile detailing around the freestanding bathtub. Updating the lighting as well as providing new Silverthorne travertine flooring gave new life to this formerly dark master bathroom.
Photograph by Julie Soefer

BELOW TOP RIGHT: Creating a master bath spa retreat led to the use of marble-clad walls and soft blue arabesque glazed tiles. Both add beautiful layers of color and movement. The marble mosaic inlay ties back to the walls and brings the freestanding bathtub to an immediate focal point.
Photograph by Colleen Duffley

BELOW BOTTOM RIGHT: Using Naval Blue, we went bold on the cabinetry and vanity. Nautical elements such as the gooseneck lights and rope-hung mirror keep the space fun. Incorporating a custom barn door lets light travel through the space while giving privacy to the shower and tub area.
Photograph by Colleen Duffley

BELOW BOTTOM LEFT: Keeping with the home's modern elements, this elegant master bathroom is all about the grey and white neutral palette—with a touch of color. The subtle silver trim on the Roman shade ties into the fixtures and art to preserve a cool and calming space.
Photograph by Julie Soefer

Interiors by Melanie King Designs, The Woodlands, TX, page 389

ABOVE TOP LEFT: A clean and pretty palette mixes metals to feel both updated and warm. Ruddy brass fixtures are repeated in the accent tile stripe around the tub and the copper wire flower sculpture on the wall. Also, throw down a zebra rug and everything looks fabulous.

ABOVE TOP RIGHT: A 1970s shell became this clean, spa-like bathroom in a natural and simple palette. Pristine glass tile in the steam shower is accented by quartz on the bench seat and threshold, which is pulled from the vanity countertops. The modern stand-alone tub sits prettily in front of the large garden window, which floods the room with natural light.

ABOVE BOTTOM: New construction made it easy to carry materials throughout this home, such as the split-face stone that makes such a statement on the wall. The modern rug pulls together all of the colors of the room. A copper tub looks out over the private backyard off the master bedroom, where there's also an outdoor shower, offering intimate privacy while convening with nature.
Photographs by Julie Soefer
Interiors by Pamela Hope Designs, Houston, TX, page 390

BELOW TOP: This graphic wall covering is utilized throughout the entire second floor stairwell gallery and hall. In the late-1800s home, the stark contrast between the classic moldings and the contemporary graphic quality of line occurring on almost every surface provides a feast for the eye. The elegant fixture choices, coupled with the creative layout of the travertine floor and handmade sandstone and marble tile on the walls, create a graphic expression that is timeless and modern.

BELOW BOTTOM LEFT: The Victoria + Albert soaking tub creates a classic silhouette in the guest bath. Matte-black finished walls recede into the background, making this small space feel much larger than it is.

BELOW BOTTOM RIGHT: The custom vanity repeats the graphic shapes, with Art Deco-inspired lighting and nickel faucets from Kallista. Made to look like a chest of drawers, the vanity is in fact a highly functional cabinet with plenty of drawer and door storage.
Photographs by Daniel Feldkamp
Interiors by Spencer Design Associates, Minneapolis, MN, page 391

ABOVE TOP: Completely unrecognizable prior to its remodel, this bathroom has luxurious elements that give it spa-like appeal. Large-format tile flooring is warmed by radiant heat below, and the custom mother-of-pearl mirrors sit above the soapstone countertop and vanity. A curbless shower in herringbone sea glass, along with a glass bathtub, provide the homeowners with two options for relaxing after a long day. Lending a soft aqua color to the space, the Palladian blue paint color sets a peaceful tone.

ABOVE BOTTOM: I went with a country farmhouse aesthetic for the bathroom of an Uptown shotgun house. Well suited to the space, design elements include the lone item salvaged from the house, a clawfoot tub, accented by an Italian ceramic pendant, a hand-woven laundry basket from South America, sconces from Circa Lighting, a vanity repurposed from an antique buffet, and a dentist cabinet from Etú Home, all showcased atop black-and-white encaustic tiles. I chose the glass-sided dentist's cabinet in place of a traditional linen closet in order to maintain the room's airiness.
Photographs by Kerri McCaffety
Interiors by Tanga Winstead Designs, New Orleans, LA, page 392

BELOW & BELOW BOTTOM RIGHT: A water leak turned into the opportunity to do a complete overhaul of the master bath—sometimes wonderful chances present themselves in unexpected ways. A beautiful chinoiserie paper is a focal point over the vanity, complemented by back-lit mirrors that emit a soft, flattering glow and turn on with just a wave of the hand. Lucite and brass handles add a fresh, modern feel to the warm wood storage. The large corner tub got ripped out in favor of an oversize walk-in shower, completely walled with quartz and patterned with a lovely accent niche and floor.

BELOW BOTTOM LEFT: This master bath was was part of a large new construction in which our firm was hired for the entire scope. Our clients wanted a timeless design, and we achieved that in the warm vanity paired with classic finishes.
Photographs by Sqft Nashville, Emily Green
Interiors by Superior Construction and Design, Lebanon, TN, page 391

LEFT : For a full bathroom remodel, we changed everything including the height of ceiling and walls. Transitional and elegant, the space is made to accommodate the homeowners into their golden years with wide-set doorways and a spacious shower. The high-gloss finish on the ceiling, chrome fixtures, and tile from Artistic Tile give the bathroom a luxury feel.
Photograph by Maksimilian Lab

BELOW: Another bathroom that we gutted down to the studs was for a Chicago couple who originally thought they wanted traditional interiors. In the end, we went with a contemporary design that the homeowners absolutely loved. Textured wall tile adds movement while custom cabinets, a luxury tub, and a large steam shower show off sleek, modern elements.
Photograph by Michael Hunter
Interiors by Total 360 Interiors, Dallas, TX, page 392

ABOVE TOP LEFT: The elegant bathtub sits on a small step-up pedestal to create drama—something also achieved by the accent wall with its water jet marble design. The cabinets are white with a grey glaze over them to accente the wood floor. I put a mosaic tile in the shower, which is on the left side of the room, and added the same mosaic on the right side to create balance.

ABOVE TOP RIGHT: This powder bath is a little jewel box—everything about it screams elegance. The mosaic marble floor and sparkling wallpaper reflect in the antique mirrored cabinetry, topped with marble and polished nickel fixtures. The sconces are finished in silverleaf, with dangling crystals that add to the drama.

ABOVE BOTTOM: This master bath has a very soft and timeless feeling. The glass tile detail in the shower mimics a waterfall and reflects the glass bead faux finish in the ceiling detail. All-custom cabinetry, gorgeous natural quartzite counters, natural stone floors and shower, and the crystal flower-shaped chandelier make this bathroom an elegant reflection of the homeowners. This space now celebrates a fresh, light palette and timeless design elements in order to create a beautiful, bright, and airy aesthetic.
Photographs by Sam Arnold, HomeAndDesignPhotography.com
Interiors by Aniko Designs, Fort Myers, FL, page 382

Design Lines Signature, Raleigh, NC, page 385

Outdoor Living

Outdoor living spaces offer a unique opportunity. They bring together the best of two worlds, where Mother Nature mingles with everyday activities. While it's normal to see families playing sports, relaxing, or dining al fresco, it's less common to see people reading, cooking, and entertaining through the seasons—these are typically conducted indoors. But they don't have to be. When crafting an outdoor living area, it's important to plan for a wide range of potential activities, but I don't focus solely on the most common outdoor fun.

To maximize spaces for near-year-round use, light and temperature control is imperative, and often requires creativity. In any design we are looking for ways to naturally cool or warm the area, which means manipulating the sunlight. I often utilize umbrellas in all shapes and sizes, whether operating from a center pole at a dining table or cantilevered over a row of lounge chairs, while fans or heaters help with temperature control.

Lori Carroll & Associates, Tucson, AZ, page 389

What I love most about designing these spaces is that nature can be used as the backdrop. For me, it provides inspiration for design, color, and form, so outdoor spaces can overflow with artistry. If strategically designed and well landscaped, an outdoor environment can provide seasonal color that creates an ever-changing canvas. Creating separate "rooms" is a fun way to look at defining the space for multiple uses. These "rooms" can be achieved with the use of elements including level changes, free-standing structures, water features, fireplaces, and gardens—the options are nearly limitless.

So the next time you're on a beautiful patio or well-designed courtyard, take it all in, and appreciate the uniqueness of outdoor spaces.

Cheers!

Judy Pickett
Design Lines Signature
Raleigh, NC
see page 385

LGB Interiors, Columbia, SC, page 389

Celaya / Soloway Interiors, Tucson, AZ, page 384

BELOW & PREVIOUS PAGE: We created an open pool area that maintains a strong sense of privacy and beauty. The secluded space is surrounded by towering conifers and lush plantings, and is outfitted with everything you'd need to lounge the day away. It connects to a full kitchen and stocked bar, and has plenty of seating with an outdoor TV. The checkerboard edge of the pool adds visual interest and plays off the vivid flowers.
Photographs by Jane Beiles Photography
Interiors by Design Lines Signature, Raleigh, NC, page 385

ABOVE TOP LEFT & BOTTOM RIGHT: A downtown Raleigh rooftop sits atop a popular development and has become an ideal entertaining space year-round. We recommended the planting of plenty of large lush grasses, hydrangeas, and bushes to offset the intense sun during the summer. The rooftop holds 50-60 people and is separated into three smaller areas, including a table that seats up to 14 guests.
Photographs by Brie Williams Photography

ABOVE TOP RIGHT & BOTTOM LEFT: When we designed the outdoor spaces of this residence, we focused on adding intimacy to the sprawling grounds that would work well for gatherings. Creating an axis, a planter leads from the family room to a covered sitting area. In another space, the eye-catching red chairs from Richard Schultz rest in the furthest-most point on the terrace and offer a feeling of privacy among the soaring trees.
Photographs by Dustin Peck Photography
Interiors by Design Lines Signature, Raleigh, NC, page 385

BELOW: The ideal climate, sweeping views, and exceptional flora and fauna are at the heart of this palatial outdoor living space. Contrasting the rugged desert landscaping, contemporary furnishings add a casual elegance, setting the stage for an engaging, al fresco dining experience. A custom fire feature becomes a work of art that fits seamlessly in the open-air design, offering warmth and ambience that will entertain guests and heat the outdoor space long after sunset.
Photograph by Bill Lesch
Interiors by Lori Carroll & Associates, Tucson, AZ, page 389

ABOVE TOP: As an extension of the interior living spaces, a well-designed backyard can have a stunning effect on the home overall. We combined intimate conversation areas, an expansive dining space, and an outdoor kitchen that provides all the amenities necessary to prepare a gourmet meal.

ABOVE TOP LEFT: This veranda was already an engaging gathering spot, complete with fantastic views and a grand fireplace. We knew that creating a seamless transition between this space and the interior was key.

ABOVE BOTTOM RIGHT: Mirroring the same casual elegance as the inside, furnishings follow the same aesthetic while satisfying the natural outdoor setting. Comfort, durability, and style are reflected in the colors, materials, and versatility of the patio.
Photographs by Bill Lesch
Interiors by Lori Carroll & Associates, Tucson, AZ, page 389

"Detailed customization can elevate even the smallest design elements. Cocktail napkins, hand towels, and candle holders become something special with highly personalized touches."
—Ginger Atherton

ABOVE: The home's exterior does not disappoint, as the journey continues with magical outdoor unicorns that give the area a regal, joyful ambience. The client's logo is emblazoned on towels, cushions, and other décor throughout the property.

FACING PAGE: An exterior foyer welcomes you to an outdoor celebration of Hollywood Regency style, where it feels like a glamorous party could begin at any moment. A bronze Italian canine statue dons a pair of Swarovski crystal collars, complemented by the long crystal tassel—the longest on the market, in fact—on the Deco-style drapery. The French-inspired console displays a Venetian antique mirror and crystal obelisks for a touch of history and elegance.
Photographs courtesy of Ginger Atherton & Associates
Interiors by Ginger Atherton & Associates, Beverly Hills, CA, page 386

ABOVE: Lush clinging ivy is one of the few original elements that remain of this seaside home after our complete remodel. An extensive loggia runs the length of the house and forces you to experience the indoor-outdoor effect of its design, with corridors that provide access to nearly every room of the house. I sourced hand-carved African wood panels and used one of the homeowners' masks as outdoor decor to extend the modern tribal vibe of the interior. Large stellate Moroccan-style light fixtures also further the overall aesthetic.

FACING PAGE TOP: Outdoor areas of this Alys Beach home include intimate courtyard spaces that surround the main house. Open to the elements, this al fresco dining spot flows into the kitchen and dining room, making outdoor entertaining a breeze. The water feature adds a calming touch to the overall ambience of the space.

FACING PAGE BOTTOM: European in style, the courtyards serve as cozy respites as the homeowners and their guests go to and from the beach, with this one providing coverage in case of inclement weather. With stunning beaches nearby, the niches are meant as spots to rest, reflect, and not detract from the surrounding natural beauty.
Photographs by Jack Gardner
Interiors by Brad Ramsey Interiors, Nashville, TN, page 383

BELOW TOP: You could easily live in this pool house pavilion, which was carefully designed to be both modern and warm, minimalistic and cozy. Indoor/outdoor fabrics are a must for durability.

BELOW BOTTOM LEFT: A great outdoor space should feel like an extension of the interiors—sometimes it's the best room in the home. This outdoor living room has a porch swing for fun, while still under cover so you can enjoy it in any weather.
This and Below Top photographs by Eric Taylor

BELOW BOTTOM RIGHT: The ceiling of this sitting room is strongly connected to the pergola outside, letting the indoors extend into the outside. A large expanse of glass slides away to provide visual and functional access to the pool. It's a perfect example of how a large space can still feel comfortable when properly scaled.
Photograph by Dana Hoff

FACING PAGE: The courtyard is created through the simplicity of architecture, helping you feel like you're a part of nature—especially with the tree growing right through the floor. This provides a great outdoor room to entertain, as well as organizes the space around it.
Photograph by Stacy Zarin Goldberg
Interiors by Rill Architects, Bethesda, MD, page 390

"Teamwork and collaboration are imperative to achieving personal and beautiful designs."
—James Rill

BELOW & FACING PAGE: Cast in-place concrete flooring extends from the main home into the screened porch, creating a continuous statement with clean, modern lines. Ghost screens and accordion doors to the main house allow for free-flowing entertaining, blurring the lines between interior and exterior spaces. The completely customizable outdoor sofas have interchangeable backs, arms, and tables so you can create the ideal environment for relaxing solo or entertaining friends and family.
Photographs by Lissa Gotwalls

Interiors by Bartone Interiors, Chapel Hill, NC , page 383

BELOW TOP: Indoors meets outdoors under the cantilever roof with unobstructed views and sounds of the evening desert. Light-colored stucco and natural stone accent walls provide a calming setting.

BELOW BOTTOM: The design of this home has the feeling of movement among nature. You'll find long, sloping roof lines against the rough mountain terrain. Whether inside or out, we wanted to capture a closeness of everyday life with nature—an example of biophilic design.
Photographs by Kurt Munger
Interiors by Celaya | Soloway Interiors, Tucson, AZ, page 384

ABOVE: We carried the use of simple, natural materials to the outdoor space. You'll see wood and stone in a natural color palette that offers a peaceful serenity. This spot is ideal for resting and conversing outdoors in any weather.
Architect: Daniel Fletcher / Architects PC
Photograph by Aaron Leitz Photography
Interiors by Carson Guest, Atlanta, GA, page 384

ABOVE: This large backyard has several seating areas, as well as a pool and fire pit, but none is more dramatic than this large cast iron table and chairs that sit just beyond the wall of French doors. The entire setup gets left out year-round, as do the custom rug and pillows, and it all holds up wonderfully.
Photograph by Suzy Gorman
Interiors by Ash Leonard Design, St. Louis, MO, page 382

BELOW: The white iron door, round windows, and coral and green terrazzo were existing in this Red Cross Show House, determining my palette and giving me a vibe to build from. The terrace felt like Dorothy Draper to me, especially with the chandeliers coming from the Eden Roc Hotel. A lot of the pieces here represent finds from the local Antique Row, such as the unused birdcage that was converted into a bar. I drew my inspiration from a fabric I chose by longtime West Palm Beach fabric and wallpaper company Bob Collins & Sons. The archival pattern Continents in turquoise was used on pillows and seat cushions and pulled together all the elements of this outdoor oasis.
Photographs by Kim Sargent

Interiors by Chad Renfro Design, Palm Beach, FL, page 384

BELOW: We worked with Mark Scott Associates for the outdoor spaces at the Newport Beach, California, home, ripping out the original backyard. The landscape architecture firm went on to win an international award for the stunning pool design. We kept the furnishings understated to capitalize on the view, and partnered with Frank Stoltz of South Coast Architects for the gazebo and stone wall.
Photographs by Robert Clark
Interiors by LGB Interiors, Columbia, SC, page 389

ABOVE: The mounted television on the stone wall makes it clear that this space was designed for entertaining and serious outdoor living. Although the cocktail tables are concrete, they have hidden casters and can be easily rolled for rearranging, as this homeowner often does for large dinner parties. All elements are intended to evoke nature—notice the wood, stone, natural fibers, and organic shapes in the planters and lighting.
Photograph by Jake Holt
Interiors by Knight Carr & Company, Greensboro, NC, page 388

ABOVE: This covered porch is an ideal spot for entertaining and dining outdoors and includes an adjacent brick patio. The space is defined by a blue rug and outdoor-ready lamp. Slate grey iron-framed furniture with pale grey cushions and blue accent pillows give the space a refined aesthetic. Ideal for family gatherings, the rectangular and round dining tables seat 10 people. Blue seat cushions, whimsical plants, and thoughtful accents complete the family's outdoor escape.
Photographs by Scott Johnson Photography
Interiors by KP Designs, Louisville, KY, page 388

BELOW: Designing living spaces has extended to the outdoors, and the one we created for a 1920s home has it all. Built for a couple who loves to entertain, the patio needed to have a space for everyone and a variety of activities. The space includes an outdoor kitchen, full bar, fireplace, TV, and a twin-bed swing. Overlooking the pool, the living area includes a heater, fan, and lush succulents. We incorporated a statue from the home's original garden near the wine rack.
Photograph by Steve Bracci Photography
Interiors by Laurie McRae Interiors, Augusta, GA, page 388

BELOW: The complete renovation of this outdoor oasis began with the reshaping of the pool deck and the relocation of the hot tub. What was once small, under-scaled tile decking was replaced with a larger, more appropriate scale of tiles. While the outdoor woven wicker may have your typical outdoor seating appearance, the material is made to withstand the harsh Texas sun on the hottest of summer days. Paired with multiple layers of performance fabric in patterns of blue and grey, each poolside entertaining section is intentionally designed to function for lounging, dining, cooking and barbecuing, and fun with friends and family.
Photographs by Michael Hunter
Interiors by Dee Frazier Interiors, Plano, TX, page 385

Interiors by Southern Studio, Cary, NC, page 391

Carson Guest, Atlanta, GA, page 384

Specialty Spaces

There are endless ways to customize a home. Some owners choose to make simple changes, such as using specific wall colors, while others want entire structure modified around their unique needs. Such opportunities allow for limitless possibilities, and as interior designers we use our creativity to design spaces that make our clients' lives easier and more comfortable.

Specialty areas allow residents to address specific interests. For instance, if homeowners want an exercise space, we can create that, which allows for treadmills and stationary bicycles to keep from crowding or changing the relaxing ambience of a master retreat or guest bedroom. Specialty spaces can serve a wide range of purposes: pet rooms, a home office, display spaces for collections, spas with saunas, massage rooms, recording or art studios, or cozy outside retreats, for instance.

These spaces are fun to design since they are unique to each owner. We once created a room specifically for a homeowner who wanted to showcase a unique, extensive antique doll collection. We installed an antique bookcase with glass doors to display the impressive collection, plus ensured that lighting precisely illuminated the dolls.

Nearly any home can be made to include a specialty space—you don't need an entire room devoted to your interest. Sometimes an outdoor spot or some custom built-ins will serve you well. Challenges do arise, which can include pinpointing an ideal location that will lend itself to privacy, and possibly dimension requirements. But don't be afraid to get creative and do some research. If you choose to use an interior designer, he or she will likely work with your budget and space.

Let this chapter inspire you to take a look around your home and see what specialty space you'd like to create.

Rita Carson Guest and John Guest
Carson Guest
Atlanta GA
see page 384

Knight Carr & Company, Greensboro, NC, page 388

Elissa Grayer Interior Design, Rye, NY, page 386

Glenna Stone Interior Design, Philadelphia, PA, page 386

BELOW & FACING PAGE: When we designed this Pebble Beach home for a power couple moving West, our goal was to create the Zen-like retirement retreat they requested on the Pacific Ocean. We knew we succeeded when the homeowners texted to tell us that the views were no less magical than those of the Australian outback they had seen while traveling. We chose quiet, simple materials that are equally beautiful and practical. Because there are dogs and cats who live there too, we selected forgiving surfaces that were beautiful and cleanable, yet tough.

PREVIOUS PAGE: The home is surrounded by a variety of indigenous grasses. It took about five months for them to become lush and full, giving the property a warm, lived-in look that the homeowners love. Expansive windows show off the stunning blue skies and sweeping ocean vistas.
Architect: Daniel Fletcher / Architects PC
Photographs by Aaron Leitz Photography
Interiors by Carson Guest, Atlanta, GA, page 384

333

"I'm most satisfied with my designs when I believe them to be well executed, timeless, beautiful, and the answer to the homeowners' dreams and needs."
—Linda Knight Carr

BELOW: We intentionally used limited upholstery in a large library space to provide access to the bookcases. The deep drawers supporting the bookshelves are designed for files of every kind: photos, clippings, memorabilia. The sliding walnut door can provide privacy yet tease the eye with a small view through the glass openings.
Photograph by Jake Holt

FACING PAGE: The Italian desk was the initial inspiration for this space, which sits immediately off the entry hall. In a small room with a pair of English club chairs and a Regency cabinet filled with antique books and bronze animal figures, this desk is an ideal place for reading, writing, or additional seating. The wall collection of framed faces was taken from *Heads*, a book dated 1704. The images represent the various passions of the soul, expressed in the human countenance.
Photograph by Mark Salisbury

Interiors by Knight Carr & Company, Greensboro, NC, page 388

"The spaces we live in day to day should reflect our individuality, our passions, our personal taste. Interior designers are honored to master this for their clients while creating spaces that are flexible to adjust to life's changes. In short, a living space is never really finished."
—Linda Knight Carr

BELOW: There is a big presence in this small room. The space is home to a small beautiful antique desk, bookcases, and a collection of the homeowners' bird mounts. Warmth and coziness are established with the rich colors in the textured grasscloth and the leather seating. For a busy doctor, this space provides a respite for reading, listening to music, and relaxing.
Photograph by Aura Marzouk

FACING PAGE: Sometimes a window view is so special that establishing the interior image that is framed can be challenging. From this window, the trunk of a live oak tree and its juxtaposition to a beautiful swimming pool is commanding. We placed an antique English partners' desk in the window and paired it with antique chairs that mimic a similar juxtaposition and create a simple yet powerful view. In addition, it provides the homeowners a wonderful place to study and work.
Photograph by Jake Holt

Interiors by Knight Carr & Company, Greensboro, NC, page 388

ABOVE: Part of a major renovation to a '90s-style home, this home office originally had a duck motif that had to go. The new owners did like the light that filtered in through the frosted glass doors, though, so we modernized that idea with simple, geometric leaded glass doors created by a local artisan.
Photograph by Jerry Portelli, Architectural Photographic Specialists
Interiors by Sesshu Design Associates, Scottsdale, AZ, page 391

BELOW TOP: This "woman cave" is where the wife can go and close the door for some quiet time—her own personal sanctuary. She liked color and an organic, natural feel, so we incorporated that with cabinetry that has a tree-with-branch motif. Even the chandelier ties into nature, effectively bringing the outdoors in.
Photograph by Jerry Portelli, Architectural Photographic Specialists

BELOW BOTTOM LEFT: Open to the great room, the wife's office can still remain a part of what's happening in the main living area. A gorgeous wool and silk rug and organic desk anchor the space, while simple bookcases allow the beautiful view to command attention.
Photograph by Jerry Portelli, Architectural Photographic Specialists

BELOW BOTTOM RIGHT: This office is all about the artwork, which we sourced from a local gallery and artist to bring in personality and color. A simple writing desk is decorated with a mineral specimen and ceramic vase that echoes the round motif in a rich eggplant hue, which the rug and desk chair also share.
Photograph by Ed Taube, Taube Photography

Interiors by Sesshu Design Associates, Scottsdale, AZ, page 391

BELOW TOP LEFT: This custom wine room was designed to also showcase the owner's bourbon collection, with the stone and reclaimed wood adding a more masculine touch. Rufty Homes helped create the room's true conversation piece: a window to the dining room next door, outfitted with storage for a collection of wine corks within the glass.

BELOW TOP RIGHT: The client requested a "happy laundry room," and it doesn't get more cheerful than sunny yellow and flowers. We started with the fabric for the window covering, based the wall and floor colors off it, added an apron-front sink, and installed plenty of storage.

BELOW BOTTOM LEFT: A mudroom must excel at containing mess and look good while doing it. The sliding barn doors conceal shoe storage, leaving the more orderly hooks on display.

BELOW BOTTOM RIGHT: What was originally a nook with a desk we turned into an orderly mudroom, with brick tile for longevity, wainscoting for architectural interest, and a cork wallcovering with a little bit of shimmer for style.
Photographs by Dustin Peck Photography
Interiors by Southern Studio, Cary, NC, page 391

ABOVE: The original artwork from our favorite local gallery accents the color palette of this home office, which we punched up with a bold grasscloth and crisp wainscoting.
Photograph by Dustin Peck Photography
Interiors by Southern Studio, Cary, NC, page 391

ABOVE LEFT: This home bar is an integral part of the living room, so everything was custom-built. A mirrored back is complemented by a quartzite waterfall countertop and V-groove wood boards on the inside.

ABOVE RIGHT: The homeowner is very into whiskey, so we made sure to include lots of display space for notable bottles. A white glass backsplash and durable quartzite counter, along with some moody navy paint, make this extension of the pantry and kitchen its own unique space.

LEFT: What would you use for the walls in a wine cellar if not cork? A barrel brick ceiling echoes the shape of the bottles, while angled display storage along the side shows off prominent vintages.

FACING PAGE TOP: This happy laundry feels like it's been there forever in this historic house, thanks to porcelain knobs on the cabinets, a retro light fixture, botanical fabric on the curtains, and celery-colored paint. The backsplash has some iridescence to it, giving the whole room a magical feel.

FACING PAGE BOTTOM: It's not so much a master closet as it is a small boutique, with plenty of glass and doors to ensure the clothes stay dust-free.
Photographs by Jessie Preza
Interiors by Lisa Gielincki Interior Design, Jacksonville, FL, page 389

"Human beings are deeply affected by the aesthetics around us. When our surroundings are customized perfectly for us, we thrive."
—Lisa Gielincki

BELOW & FACING PAGE: When we worked with a homeowner who is 100-percent Irish, we created an authentic-looking traditional Irish pub in his existing basement. The look had to include rustic oak, dark woods, textured paint, brick walls, and a tin-tile ceiling, all layered to make it look like it was added over time. The space also had to have practical finishes to withstand two children under 10, two dogs, and two cats, plus beer spills and possible wet floors due to the patio entry.

Made from red oak, the wainscot, bar, and cabinetry are custom-designed with an ebonized finish, all milled and built on-site. The bar's steel top is acid-splashed for an aged aesthetic and finished with a clear coat for durability. The rail runs from the bar to the dart board corner, providing a place to rest a pint along one entire wall.

We painted all of the crown, door, and window trim in a color that would blend in with the mortar and help add to the darker atmosphere in a pub setting. The double-sliding entry doors are made of reclaimed wood.
Contractor: Oxford Contracting
Photographs by Quentin Penn-Hollar, QPH Photo
Interiors by Kathy Corbet Interiors, Richmond, VA, page 387

ABOVE TOP: An historic home on the shores of Lake Minnetonka had an unusual space oddly placed at the end of a great room which the owners had no idea how to incorporate into the overall design. The solution was simple:, turn it into a bar. The owners now use it as a place to enjoy rare wines, toast in celebration, or savor a cigar. The room was trimmed out in millwork and the walls and ceiling were lacquered in a high-gloss black Sherwin Williams color. The adjoining space sports a poker table and chairs upholstered in a handsome wool plaid and leather combo. The room is also home to a cozy grouping of chairs surrounding a statement-making leopard ottoman, trimmed in red leather with nailhead. The final touch was a one-of-a-kind bold art piece. This room was honored with the top National Award Design by IDS.

ABOVE BOTTOM: After a major remodel, the traditional bones of this bar and library space remained. The knackered wood was fully restored to a gorgeous luster. New rugs, furnishings, art, and accessories were added. A few reupholstered antique pieces were a graceful complement to new modern barstools that were covered in a sumptuous Ralph Lauren velvet. Curated pieces throughout give this space its elegant distinction.
Photographs by Bill Diers

Interiors by Kamarron Design, Inc., Minneapolis, MN, page 387

FACING PAGE TOP: A dated lower-level entertainment space was ready for a refresh. Wide-plank hardwood replaced an unfashionable multi-colored slate. A shined coat of Venetian plaster troweled onto the ceiling helped reflect light into the space. A talented artist, Melinda Bender, covered the walls and ceiling in "graffiti" of the family's names, birthdates, other important dates, and phrases, making this awkward corner became the perfect space for a few pinball machines. The black-and-white striped velvet panel adds sophistication and can be removed in case they ever switch out the pinball games. Custom art from the Netherlands adds a pop of color and serves as the backdrop to the ping-pong table made of solid walnut with a handsome leather net and paddles. **This room was honored with the top National Award Design by IDS.**

FACING PAGE BOTTOM: On the edge of the shore, this one-of-a-kind Lake Minnetonka boat house is a relaxing recreational spot. The tranquil sounds of the waves crashing against the shore make this a magical haven for family and friends. Original wood clads the walls and a padded upholstered wall was added to display custom-framed photographs that the client had taken on enchanting trips. Striking embroidered upholstery enhances the comfy rocking chairs while an American Leather sleeper enveloped in a neutral stripe encourages guests to kick back and stay awhile. **This room was honored with the top National Award Design by IDS.**
Photographs by Bill Diers
Interiors by Kamarron Design, Inc., Minneapolis, MN, page 387

ABOVE: Beautiful wainscoting is a hallmark of this cherry-paneled bar, which also sports a custom wood bartop with drink rail and quartz lower counter with sink and built-in beverage center.
General contracting by TZ of Madison, Inc.
Photographs by Marcia Hansen Photographic Company

FACING PAGE: Label-forward wine racks are a slick feature of this custom wine cellar, which has a counterpart in the contemporary bar. A mix of modern and traditional elements are highlighted by the beveled glass backsplash tile, backlit quartz shelves, and dramatic cabinetry in Sherwin Williams Naval.
Collaboration with Fig Interiors, general contracting by Buss Construction, Inc.
Photographs by S. Cole Photography
Interiors by Curran Cabinetry & Design, Madison, WI, page 385

ABOVE: The rich hues of the coffered ceiling complement all the sparkling glassware and the bronze mirror backsplash in the bar area, which comes in handy while sports games are playing on the seven televisions. A built-in refrigerator, microwave, and dishwasher make it easy to serve snacks and clean up afterward.

FACING PAGE TOP: A huge Clemson football fan wanted a room where he could host large viewing parties, and you won't miss a play from anywhere in the room. The furnishings are all custom, with movie theater chairs that recline and barstools that swivel so there's never an obstructed view. Autographed sports memorabilia is given prominent placement on the walls.

FACING PAGE BOTTOM: The doors open completely to the patio, which overlooks the Intracoastal Waterway and the home's pool. A stone fireplace keeps it cozy for outdoor game-watching, while a large table can seat even more fans.
Built by Babb Custom Homes.
Photographs by Scott Smallin
Interiors by Legacy Interiors, Myrtle Beach, SC, page 388

> "Nothing compares to having a client enter their new house and hear them say, 'Wow, this feels like home.'"
> –Lucy Emory Hendricks

ABOVE TOP: This foyer of a Frank Lloyd Wright home in St. Louis needed to do more than just sit pretty. The family operates vineyards in California and they often host wine tastings for professional and personal events. We wanted this larger-scale foyer to provide additional space for guests to sample wine flights and, should a guest want to linger and sample more, feel more than comfy in the dramatic wing chairs flanking the table.

ABOVE BOTTOM LEFT: Clients will no doubt hear my mantra "start with art" from the outset of a project, as I love using something from their own collection to ground the design. In this home, we ran the rule writ large and used their collection as a whole as our grounding point for the entire interior. We created a gallery-like feel with well-lit, wider, and longer hallways providing due space for each piece in the formidable collection. We also used custom bronze-framed glass walls so the pieces are visible from multiple sightlines, such as the bronze sculpture *Flowers* by Donald Baechler, seen beyond the glass.
Photographs by Erik Johnson

ABOVE BOTTOM RIGHT: This well-stocked bar cart would make even Andy himself proud; especially when used as the anchor to the great *Bighorn Ram*, from his Endangered Species series.
Photograph by Kevin Allen

Interiors by Lori Graham Design + HOME, Washington, DC, page 388

BELOW: Lucious mohair velvet on E. Saarinen's signature Womb chair, which sits atop The Rug Company's iconic Papillion silk rug, makes this home office reading nook all the more inviting.
Photograph by Erik Johnson
Interiors by Lori Graham Design + HOME, Washington, DC, page 388

"I love creating the texture of a space—that slicing and dicing of cultural, historical, geographical, intellectual, and artistic references that make a space multi-dimensional."
—Lori Graham

ABOVE & FACING PAGE TOP: The homeowner was intent on creating a sophisticated yet family-friendly home for his four children at this stunning property in the grand tradition of Westchester and Greenwich estates. The homeowner's taste for sophisticated furniture and unique finishes was a perfect fit for Elissa Grayer's signature style of "classic luxury for modern living."
Photographs by John Bessler

FACING PAGE BOTTOM: For this pied-à-terre, a New York City executive wanted us to create a space that not only serves his need for a serene escape from his weekday business dealings, but also acts as a metropolitan landing pad for his entire family.
Photograph by Regan Wood
Interiors by Elissa Grayer Interior Design, Rye, NY, page 386

"Many hands go into pulling together a beautifully crafted room. The trick is to make it look seamless."
— Elissa Grayer

"Our special skill is not mind-reading. It's listening to and understanding what homeowners want—that often feels more like mind-reading to our clients."
—Michelle Lynne

BELOW: For an attorney's home office, we created a distinctly masculine space. The homeowner had standard white built-ins on the opposite wall, but they didn't fit his edgy style, took up too much space, and weren't fully utilized. We pulled them out and created the unique wall shelves that you see now. The credenza behind the desk offers storage while the natural shape of the cowhide rug counteracts all the hard, angular lines in the room to bring balance. Greenery dots the interior, which reflects the family's love of the outdoors.

FACING PAGE: The lady of the house needed an efficient home office to run the busy household. We layered using tone-on-tone in blacks, greys, whites, and ivories, plus textured wallpaper that gives dimension. To keep the sitting area feeling more open, we used an ottoman instead of two chairs. The fresh puff of pink is a pretty reminder that this is a woman's territory.
Photographs by Matti Gresham Photography
Interiors by ML Interiors Group, Dallas, TX , page 389

ABOVE TOP: Anchored by a sumptuous Bernhardt snakeskin desk, this home office exudes personal distinction with an eclectic twist. I curated this full-time home office with collected antique pieces, richly colored art glass, and strategically placed personal mementos. Fun and functional, it perfectly embodies the homeowner's vintage rock 'n roll style.

ABOVE BOTTOM: This home office was designed with a feminine flair featuring pink and pastel colors. Furnished with antiques, I recycled and reupholstered the chairs in sophisticated fabrics. The tall flower art piece was commissioned for this space by artist, Shelley McCoy, to inspire beauty and creativity.

FACING PAGE: My client's love for the vast skies and strikingly stark beauty of Scotland and the American Southwest inspired the blue, green and copper-toned color scheme in the two-story great room and throughout the home for this busy father of three. Accents include a blue soapstone-topped metal console in the gracious foyer displaying a set of burled-wood boxes and a collection of pheasant feathers in a copper trophy cup, hammered copper coffee tables, and touches of natural elements to evoke the beauty of the Scottish countryside and to provide comfortable functionality for the whole family.
Photographs by J. Totten Photo

Interiors by Home by Hattan, Nashville, TN, page xx

ABOVE: A comfortable home office was a must for clients whose careers sometimes lead them to work in the evenings or on weekends. Because the office is adjacent to the entry and visible to guests, we created a stylish space with custom built-ins and a beautiful fireplace. The slightly moody color palette sets it apart from the rest of the home.

FACING PAGE TOP: The combination laundry and mudroom works hard for the whole family, including their beloved dog, who claims her very own custom-designed crate integrated into the cabinetry that houses the laundry sink. The pull-down faucet doubles as her shower at bath time, while the bench features storage and offers a place to remove shoes—and wipe paws.

FACING PAGE BOTTOM LEFT: A combination of shelving, cubbies, and ventilated cabinets holds everything from boots and sports equipment to jackets and coats.

FACING PAGE BOTTOM RIGHT: The laundry area also contains plentiful storage along with a pull-out drying rack and a wide countertop for sorting and folding. A clever pocket door closes this space away from the rest of the home.
Photographs by Rebecca McAlpin Photography
Interiors by Glenna Stone Interior Design, Philadelphia, PA, page 386

ABOVE TOP: Architectural planning from Alexander Design Group and several small but important details help to faithfully recreate a traditional English pub, such as the brass rail footrest, paneling on the walls, and dark ceiling for a cavernous feel. There's a wet bar and dishwasher drawer for cleaning barware, as well as a built-in beverage refrigerator. The beveled mirror backsplash adds a bit of light and reflection to the space, which was created with help from Fred Nordahl Construction, Inc. Library chairs provide a place to get cozy and are supplemented by a table from a whiskey barrel. There are even hooks under the bar for hanging up your bags.
Photograph by Spacecrafting

ABOVE BOTTOM: These homeowners love to travel and collect wine from various regions, so I gave them a truly spectacular way to showcase their collection with help from Fred Nordahl Construction, Inc. Stacked three rows deep with mirrors on the back to give an infinity illusion, the custom refrigerated wine cabinet can hold up to 300 bottles. When this hockey family is ready to watch a game, the motorized TV pops up from its recessed spot in the bar.
Photograph by Alyssa Lee Photography
Interiors by M Gilbertson Design, Eden Prairie, MN, page 390

BELOW TOP: Clean lines and rich colors define this masculine office. The homeowner includes two pieces of art that show off his favorite places, one a painting of Asheville, North Carolina, and the other, Newport Beach, California.
Photograph by Robert Clark

BELOW BOTTOM: We turned a not-so-exciting living space into the ultimate man cave. It offers a place to play cards, a shuffleboard table, and a sitting area by the fireplace for cocktails and conversation. There is also an impressive guitar collection signed by legendary musicians.
Photograph by Dustin Peck

Interiors by LGB Interiors, Columbia, SC, page 389

BELOW: Rather than a place to shut herself away, this Realtor's home office is her family's gathering space. Her husband often joins her at the oversized desk, and her two boys practice music by the tiled fireplace. The owner initially didn't want a dramatic look, but 25-foot ceilings practically demand bold choices. Now it's everyone's favorite room in the house. My mother, Marie Rios, is the owner of Troo Home Staging, and she's my partner in the finishing touches once the design is completed.
Photograph by Keith Trigaci
Interiors by Patrice Rios Interiors, Austin, TX, page 390

BELOW TOP: The family didn't want traditional theater seating for their movie room, but rather a large sectional that encourages snuggling up and sprawling out, and feels like you're falling into a cloud. C-tables can be moved around to hold drinks, snacks, and other accessories. Painting the walls a moody blue made sense not only from a practical standpoint, but it also elicits an emotional response that this is a cozy escape.

BELOW BOTTOM LEFT: An animal-hide rug gives this home office some real cowboy flair, while the overall design is masculine yet clean and uncluttered. We painted the doors going into the room black to accentuate the palette—you can never go wrong with black and white.

BELOW BOTTOM RIGHT: Built-ins are a great place to add color and create excitement in a room. The rug picks up on the blue in the bookcases, while oversized art feels scaled just right with the tall ceilings. A fun light fixture sets off the wood-paneled ceiling and ties the home office together.
Photographs by Miro Dvorscak

Interiors by B. de Vine Interiors, Houston, TX, page 383

BELOW TOP & BOTTOM LEFT: For an entryway, I wanted to create an urban, soulful vibe, which I achieved by using bold, detailed, dominant artwork. The interior wall consists of three different paint colors, which complements the artwork and becomes a focal point. The addition of furniture, an area rug, and decorative objects creates a stylish and inviting entrance.

BELOW BOTTOM RIGHT: This statement-making stairway has a Zen-like quality from the large Buddha heads, which also add character and style. I used a wall paint technique from a mixture of three colors, set against the dark hardwood floors for the perfect contrast.
Photographs by Apollo's Bow Photography

Interiors by KCL-IDESIGN, LLC, Mauldin, SC, page 388

ABOVE: I brought a modern twist to a traditional gentleman's barber suite, relying on vintage-inspired furniture and clean, geometric lines. The black, white, grey, and red palette immediately establishes a retro feel.
Photograph by Gethro Genius, Quantized Pixels
Interiors by Sanctuary Rooms, Glenarden, MD, page 390

ABOVE: Set in a designer show house, this creative space reflects the idea of a female world explorer who would return to her office to unwind. The space features her "finds" and plans for future excursions. The palette is soft with brown, grey neutrals, and blush pinks. A backdrop of a sweet diamond-dot patterned wallpaper adds color and interest to the room. The writing desk is both functional and pretty with its broomstick chair, while a large vintage cabinet holds books and global treasures. The comfy antique chaise is covered with a warm, textured fabric, perfect for an afternoon nap. The pretty-in-pink window treatments have embroidered linen fabric framed by geometric-pattern drapery panels. Travel and nature-inspired art complete the home office of our "explorer."
Photographs by Accent Photography
Interiors by KP Designs, Louisville, KY, page 388

Interiors by ML Interiors Group, Dallas, TX , page 389

Total 360 Interiors, Dallas, TX, page 392

Custom Furniture

Designing a room can be a bit like completing a puzzle—everything has its place, and if something is missing or out of sync, it's obvious. Oftentimes custom furniture is necessary to achieve a perfect fit, or to complete the puzzle, if you will. Every piece has to make sense in the room, and nothing should be forced.

We love using custom furniture in our designs because of the freedom it provides. We don't have to spend time and energy hunting for what we want; instead, we create it. This allows us to focus on our projects and construct the furniture for our specific purposes. Customized pieces also allow for limitless possibilities when interpreting a homeowner's lifestyle and preferences. Our individual styles are reflected in each of our projects while incorporating the clients' personalities. We focus on accomplishing this in a thoughtful, interesting way, and that may mean making furniture from scratch.

As designers, it's important that we stay open-minded, which means embracing the fact that sometimes a mass-produced piece of furniture works well in a room. If it looks great, we go for it. But we never cheat the room—and neither should you if you design a space in your own home. There is this notion that custom furniture has to be expensive, and that's not necessarily true. Unique, custom furniture is always an option regardless of budget. We strive for high-quality as opposed to high-dollar, and sometimes that means simplicity.

Our hope is that you read these pages and begin to notice the curves, contours, and textures on furniture and how it interacts with the room, and that it deepens your appreciation for well-designed pieces.

Nancy Black, Brent Willmott, and Kat Black
Total 360 Interiors, Inc.
Dallas, TX
see page 392

Kamarron Design, Inc, Minneapolis, MN, page 387

Kathy Corbet Interiors, Richmond, VA, page 387

Curran Cabinetry & Design, Madison, WI, page 385

BELOW TOP: We packed loads of storage and functionality into a hallway office: a pull-out printer shelf, pull-out work surface extension, and under-window seating with hidden file drawers. The cherry Shaker-style cabinetry presents a neat and tidy face to those passing by. Collaboration with Laurie Driscoll Interiors.

BELOW BOTTOM: A traditional home office is elevated through a custom wood fireplace surround, bookcase, and executive desk. Matching wainscoting and trim detail complement the style of the home. General contracting by Thiede Construction.

FACING PAGE TOP: This maple wine bar has an integrated tasting station supported by a custom corbel and half-moon tabletop in a grey stain. Integral lighting supports the label-forward wine racks, which can hold up to 108 bottles. Lower cabinets provide extra storage and a place for accessories. General contracting by Thiede Construction.

FACING PAGE BOTTOM: This home theater's wet bar is comprised of maple Shaker-style cabinets with a grey stain. A mosaic glass tile backsplash and natural stone countertop with a honed finish pull everything together. General contracting by Thiede Construction.

Photographs by Marcia Hansen Photographic Company
Interiors by Curran Cabinetry & Design, Madison, WI, page 385

TOP LEFT: We chose a 60-by-60-inch custom-stained coffee table in a weathered oak to coordinate with the nearby dining table. Its two-tier design allows room for everybody in the family to gather and put their feet up or eat a meal while watching the big game.
Photograph by Unique Exposure Photography

TOP RIGHT: We designed a highly functional home office while creating plenty of storage and interest. The original windows stayed and we built around them, allowing for natural light to pour in. Lights above the windows serve as accents and offer extra lighting for late-night work. Two desk areas allow for plenty of workspace, and low-slung seating works as a comfortable resting place that doesn't clutter the floorplan.

BOTTOM LEFT: At 72-by-72 inches, this beast of a dining table had to be carried in by six men and assembled on-site. Its white-oak neutral tone and traditionally shaped base allow the rest of the bold decorating choices to shine. Notice the hot pink wallpaper on the back of the built-in china cabinet, faux-fur bench, and zebra-striped chairs.
Photograph by Michael Hunter Photography

BOTTOM RIGHT: In a contemporary home that was already filled with organic design elements, a concrete coffee table served as the ideal solution. It withstands the busy household that includes five children, three dogs, and two parents who manage to keep it all together. The grey concrete, light-colored rug, and grey upholstery on the sofas keep the space light and airy among the mayhem. The custom pouf under the table is perfect for the Mrs. to pull out and prop up her feet.
This and Top Right photographs by Emery Davis Photography

Interiors by ML Interiors Group, Dallas, TX , page 389

TOP LEFT: We used an eclectic mix of wood, metal, glass, and stone that satisfies both classic and contemporary styles for this dining room. Curved design elements convey a modern flair, while earthy tones and natural materials give the setting an informal edge.

TOP RIGHT: Mixing unique patterns, textures, and materials can dramatically change the look of a room, as illustrated in this fireplace façade. Combining different elements to create a cohesive look starts with choosing a primary material and building on contrasting colors, finishes, and surfaces that blend well together.

BOTTOM LEFT: With the fireplace as a focal point, this space starts with neutral tones, relying on unique shapes and textures to provide visual interest. We designed it to fit the needs of a busy couple, with comfortable seating, easy-to-clean surfaces, and simple accessories.

BOTTOM RIGHT: Modern style has its appeal, but moderating the clean lines and sleek surfaces requires bold accents to add personality. In this space, the emerald green fireplace and vibrant artwork add touches of color without overwhelming the overall design.
Photographs by Bill Lesch
Interiors by Lori Carroll & Associates, Tucson, AZ, page 389

BELOW: For a custom butler's pantry, the homeowner wanted to include a Kegerator and desired a special sink that would double as an ice bucket while entertaining. The space is a typical pass-through room between the kitchen and the dining room, but we made it special by adding the upper cabinets and display shelf. We used cut-pebble tile for the countertop and sink, and a special substrate with grooves was used for the barrel shape. The backsplash is a multi-layer decorative finish with a metallic Venetian plaster base and a faux leather stenciled fretwork and nail-head pattern.
Builder: Jones Homes
Decorative artist: Art To Di For
Photographs by Quentin Penn-Hollar, QPH Photo
Interiors by Kathy Corbet Interiors, Richmond, VA, page 387

> *"Becoming an influence in someone's environment is a privilege."*
> —Linda Knight Carr

ABOVE LEFT: While adding storage in a dining room appointed with English 18th-century furniture, I introduced a lighter mood. Minding restrictions of space, I designed a custom cabinet perfectly proportioned to store the clients' china. The painted finish is layered in multiple shades of cream and umber, while the top has been faux marbled.

ABOVE RIGHT: In a bright contemporary seating space with a grouping of four facing chairs, there needed to be an ottoman with a perfect circumference and height for the chair seats. To make this piece more playful, I connected with a source that makes Lucite furniture legs and had the ottoman built with five of these legs and a fabric that exuded the fun feeling of the space.
Photographs by Aura Marzouk

Interiors by Knight Carr & Company, Greensboro, NC, page 388

ABOVE TOP: Designed in collaboration with Brian Fireman—we actually went to graduate school together—this table is a statement piece defined by a powder-coated steel base and massive walnut four-piece top. It's surrounded by Series 7 chairs and stands in front of a Radio House sofa, with a Roll and Hill chandelier and motorcycle art adding a bit of edge.

ABOVE BOTTOM LEFT: Hidden structural steel supports the maple bookshelves designed specifically for this home library. Their industrial vibe is softened by a pair of white Papa Bear chairs.

ABOVE BOTTOM RIGHT: Designed in collaboration with BDDW, this D-shaped dining table has a curving live edge to accommodate antique rosewood and walnut chairs. A walnut and leather bench, also by BDDW, seats more guests along the straight edge. A bespoke Cibola Shallot chandelier from Scabetti artfully elevates fine bone china.
Photographs by Stacy Zarin Goldberg
Interiors by Design Milieu, Washington, DC, page 385

BELOW TOP: Centered around the eye-catching Christopher Martin painting, the design of this living room includes blue, grey, and yellow tones. The striking Roche Bobois chair was custom-made with yellow leather.
Photograph by Matti Gresham

BELOW BOTTOM: When we created a dining nook for a family with young children and pets, it had to be high-functioning and durable. We chose resistant materials for the drapes and made sure everything worked well in high-traffic areas, including the leather banquette and white-oak table. At the bottom of the banquette we crafted a doggy door that leads directly outside—a fun feature that makes this space especially unique.
Photograph by Maksimilian Lab
Interiors by Total 360 Interiors, Dallas, TX, page 392

BELOW: This chic play on pastels remains grown-up thanks to steel, marble, and glass accents and traditional patterns like houndstooth. The result is a light and airy room with midcentury modern inspiration.
Photograph by Gethro Genius, Quantized Pixels
Interiors by Sanctuary Rooms, Glenarden, MD, page 390

ABOVE: Mitchell Gaudet's *Love Story* is a custom art installation that steals the show in this master bedroom. Made of sand-cast glass, each page contains one word that, when strung together, read like a book and tell the story of the couple who live here. I designed the floating coffee bar just below the artwork, with a pattern that mimics the look of the coffered ceiling. A design collaboration between Erica Larkin Gaudet and myself, the bed features pearlized pleated leather topped with custom bedding.

RIGHT: When my client first asked me to find a glass bathtub—she had seen one while traveling—I didn't know that it would end up being an engineering feat. Difficult to create but well worth the effort, the powder-coated custom stainless tub is supported by the pony wall and has double panes of glass that can withstand a great deal of pressure when full. The bottom of the tub was created to be level with the floor for a seamless look.
Photographs by Kerri McCaffety
Interiors by Tanga Winstead Designs, New Orleans, LA, page 392

"Many of my ideas come from problem-solving specific requests, but the best things pop into my head when I'm thinking about something else entirely. Sometimes rules are made to be broken."
—Tanga Winstead

Meet the Designers

Gina Roth
Abode Interior Design • San Antonio, Texas • 210.269.3351
Energetic, vivacious, enthusiastic—these words describe not just Gina V. Roth's designs, but the designer herself. From traditional to funky to contemporary, Gina and her team have been creating spaces since 2013 that function beautifully and reflect the taste and preferences of those who live and work there. After living for several years in Europe, Gina returned to the States and trained as a True Color Expert with Maria Killam, now using her system of Understanding Undertones to help clients navigate the right color palette for their interiors and exteriors. Embracing a broad range of design styles, the Abode team is passionate about capturing the uniqueness of each client.
See her work on pages 105, 214, 254
and at www.myabodedesign.com

Nadia Subaran & Kelly Emerson
Aidan Design Kitchen Form + Function • 8935 Brookville Rd, Silver Spring, MD 20910 • 301.320.8735
Creativity is at the forefront of every project at Aidan Design. The Maryland-based firm began with co-founder and co-owner Nadia Subaran, who brings more than 20 years of design innovation to the table. Along with showroom manager and designer Kelly Emerson and their devoted team, Nadia stands firm on her mantra that "form follows function." Specializing in kitchens, she practically approaches projects and engages homeowners along the way. With a goal of attaining structure and beauty, projects from Aidan Design reveal organized, balanced spaces that reflect clients' lifestyles and interests. Nadia holds a Bachelor of Architecture degree from The Cooper Union for the Advancement of Art and Science. Kelly has a Bachelor of Fine Arts degree in interior design from George Washington University.
See her work on pages 112-115, 182, 183, 276, 277
and at www.aidandesign.com

Ami Austin
Ami Austin Interior Design LLC • Memphis, TN 38103 • 901.458.4255
Award-winning designer Ami Austin founded her namesake firm in 2004, debuting a sophisticated and intriguing evolution of style built on a wealth of design knowledge and unique, creative, comfortable, and functional designs. Ami has a wide-ranging talent for transforming homes to suit the personalities and lifestyles of her clients by adapting interiors with design elements sourced throughout the U.S. and abroad. She specializes in unique custom upholstery, accessories, and objects d'art. A bespoke line of merchandise personally designed by Ami, under the brand name Parker Lauren by Ami Austin, is also showcased at her Memphis studio.
See her work on pages 38, 39, 179, 186, 187, 230, 231, 288
and at www.amiaustininteriors.com

Aniko Brittingham ASID, Green AP, NCIDQ
Aniko Design • 15961 McGregor Boulevard, Unit 4, Fort Myers, FL 33908 • 239.994.8208
Principal and lead designer Aniko Brittingham has an extensive background in marketing, public relations, and design, and used that vast experience to create her successful studio. The philosophy of her design is about the client: who they are and how to best represent their lives. She builds off their needs and desires to create unique, exceptional interiors that reflect the owner's personality, all the while maintaining continuity by directing the project through the process. Her full-service design firm offers complete CAD capabilities for interior detailing as well as a full library of furnishings, accessories, and window treatments.
See her work on pages 64, 65, 252, 305
and at www.anikodesign.com

Aisling "Ash" Leonard
Ash Leonard Design • St. Louis, MO • 314.642.4847
Having grown up and trained in Dublin, Ireland, Ash Leonard's taste and aesthetic is informed by the clean, defined lines typical of Dublin's Georgian architecture. Also prevalent is the presence of family, which is often reflected in her use of heirloom pieces to truly personalize a space. Together with clients in Dublin, Boston, and—since 2010—St. Louis, Ash has created spaces that are functional and beautiful while embodying the clients themselves; workspaces to encourage their productivity, entertainment spaces to enhance their social lives, and living spaces to simplify their day-to-day lives. She's known for bringing a fresh perspective and new ideas to problems clients might have thought insolvable, changing their homes in ways they never even imagined.
See her work on pages 146, 147, 322
and at www.ashleonarddesignllc.com

Carolyn Blum
B. de Vine Interiors • 122 Vintage Park Boulevard, Suite D, Houston, Texas 77070 • 832.717.0299
Though B. de Vine has been Houston's go-to showroom and furniture store for the last seven years, Carolyn Blum has been flexing her design muscles for more than 20. The brick-and-mortar space allows shoppers to actually see, touch, and try out pieces that may end up in their homes. Carolyn and her team of professionals use their expertise to offer full-scale interior design services, including mock-up layouts so it's easier for a client to envision what the end result might really be—and the answer is always "divine."
See her work on pages 103, 207, 291, 365
and at www.bdevineinteriors.com

Monique Sabatino
Balanced Interiors • Narragansett, RI 02882 • 401.640.1591
Monique Sabatino has always loved transforming ordinary spaces into extraordinary ones. The University of Rhode Island and RISD graduate followed her heart by opening her own design company, and now she channels that passion so that the end result surpasses her clients' expectations. As its name suggests, Balanced Interiors is all about being in tune with nature's rhythms to create balance in a home. Monique uses the right amount of textures, shapes, and colors to create a smooth transition between indoor and outdoor spaces, always integrating nature's beauty and elements into her designs. By being environmentally conscious, Monique believes she can make not just beautiful rooms, but a beautiful world.
See her work on pages 88, 89, 212, 261
and at www.balancedinteriors.com

Kristin Bartone
Bartone Interiors • 121 South Estes Drive, Suite 100, Chapel Hill, NC 27514 • 919.679.2303
With the goal of creating beautiful spaces that enhance a person's overall well-being, Kristin Bartone and her experienced team blend creativity with science, delivering a restorative sanctuary with every project. As a young girl, Kristin's interest in design was ignited by working in her father's custom furniture-making studio. This attention to design details, combined with a personal investment in health and wellness, results in innovative design solutions that makes her clients' lives easier, more enjoyable, and more beautiful every time.
See her work on pages 236, 237, 318, 319
and at www.bartoneinteriors.com

Brad Ramsey
Brad Ramsey Interiors • 4119 Hillsboro Pike, Nashville, TN 37215 • 615.746.7364
For Brad Ramsey, interior design is all about people. He began his namesake firm, Brad Ramsey Interiors, in 2012 with a commitment to connecting to his clients. The full-service, Nashville-based design studio has taken projects of all sizes, from commercial buildings to small-space remodels. Skilled at listening, Brad tailors each design to his clients' wishes and lifestyles and adapts his cool, clean, modern appeal to suit the project at hand. With each collaboration, he spends time getting to know his clients: not just their design preferences but who they are as people. Knowing and understanding the homeowners is the only way to create the customized, ideal living spaces that Brad has become known for.
See his work on pages 52, 53, 190, 191, 250, 314, 315
and at www.bradramseyinteriors.com

Brett Seidl
Brett Nicole Interiors • Frisco, TX 75034 • 713.408.1709
Brett Seidl believes interior design shouldn't be stiff or unlivable. Instead, she draws on everything from simple and clean modernism to mix-and-match Bohemian to bring her clients' unique perspectives to life. After having lived and studied in a variety of cities and countries, all of which have dramatically influenced her design aesthetic, Brett is personally drawn to an eclectic style of neutral palette foundations layered with bold splashes of color and organic textures, interesting furnishings, and, of course, just a little bit of whimsy and fun. She has designed rooms, offices, and homes from California to New York, but she's always staring at paint chips, dreaming up new wall treatments, or pouring over the latest patterns for her next project.
See her work on pages 76, 77
and at www.brettnicoleinteriors.com

Catherine Talkington
Ca'Shae Interior Design • Roswell, GA 30075 • 770.315.9432
Catherine Talkington is always driven by the same goal: that her clients love their space. Whether the undertaking is a single room or an entire home, new construction or a renovation, bold contemporary or classic traditional, Catherine continually strives to help her clients generate a new love and appreciation for their homes. Even with decades of experience to rely upon, Catherine still views each new project as an opportunity for innovation. By applying timeless design principles and blending architectural details with interior furnishings, the resulting space is a true reflection of the homeowner and how they live.
See her work on pages 4, 102, 148, 149, 259
and at www.cashaeinteriordesign.com

John Guest & Rita Carson Guest, FASID
Carson Guest Inc • 1776 Peachtree Road NW, Suite 280S, Atlanta, GA 30309 • 404.873.3663
Rita Carson Guest has never known a life without the influence of color and design. Those elements have always been present, including the early years when she used folders to carefully plan houses for her paper dolls. That spark led her to pursue a degree in interior design, and eventually, to establish Carson Guest, an interior design firm where she is the president and director of design, with her founding partner and COO John Guest. Together, the pair operates their Atlanta-based firm with a love for classic design, whether modern or traditional. They focus on function and thoughtful living. Carson Guest homes are comfortable, beautiful, and inspire the people who live within them.
See their work on pages 12,56,57,138,139,251,321,330,332,333, Front cover
and at www.carsonguest.com

Esthela J. Celaya
Celaya | Soloway Interiors • 7230 North La Cañada Drive, Tucson, Arizona 85718 • 520.219.6302
Designing is an organic process for Esthela Celaya, a trait that is evidenced by how comfortable and natural her projects feel. As the head of interior design at Tucson-based Celaya | Soloway Interiors, Esthela connects her design to the home's architecture, resulting in spaces that have a natural quality. This approach makes sense given the fact that Esthela has an innate interest in art and design. Although her credentials include formerly holding the presidency for the local chapters of ASID and NKBA and a B.S. in interior design, Esthela first began drawing at age 2 on her father's drafting table in Mexico. She's now a 20-plus-year veteran of the industry who brings a cohesive, detailed passion to the firm that clients love.
See her work on pages 3,58,59,164,203,294,307,320
and at www.soloway-designs.com

Cheryl Fosdick
CF Design LTD • 230 East Superior Street, Suite 102, Duluth, MN 55802 • 218.722.1060
A background in architecture informs Cheryl's current designs, which tell a distinct story for each person that inhabits them. An intimate relationship between site and space, with daylight reigning supreme, is the foundation. Simplicity is worth the extra effort, Cheryl believes, along with nothing designed in haste is designed well. From cabins and cottages to family compounds, Cheryl and her team—there's a satellite office in Wisconsin—work hard to ensure that their houses not only speak to the clients' comforts, motivations, and strengths, but also impart their stories. Knowing that homes represent a person's values as well as embody their heritage and culture make them an opportunity to celebrate both the individual and their community. A well-designed and well-made home improves many lives, in many ways.
See her work on pages 99,109,152,153,290
and at www.cfdesignltd.com

Chad Renfro
Chad Renfro Design, LLC • 277 Royal Poinciana Way, Palm Beach, FL 33480 • 561.503.3128
From Mexico to Montana, Tulsa to West Palm Beach, the Bahamas and beyond, Chad Renfro has been applying his expert use of color, texture, and finishes professionally since 2007. Working closely with his clients in all aspects of design, furniture, and finish detail, Chad finds the best sources for quality materials and workmanship. He has the innate ability to transition from traditional to modern, depending upon the space as well as the style the client is seeking. Each design has a seamless cohesiveness, integrating layers that impart an understated timelessness that may be rich in history, depending upon the structure's lineage and client's aesthetic, yet reinterpreted for present day and beyond. Chad's depth of understanding of space, scale, and proportion is impeccable for reconfiguring spaces and creating optimum flow, speaking to how the client lives and entertains.
See his work on pages 66,67,244,323,Front flap
and at www.chadrenfrodesign.com

Chandra Stone
Chandra Stone, Interior Design • 1302 Waugh Drive, Unit 329, Houston TX 77019 • 713.622.4455
Several factors led to Chandra Stone exploring interior design as a career, from sewing her own clothes to working in the fabric department of a dime store to reupholstering a chair in faux fur. But it wasn't until college that she began studying it in earnest, beginning with a career in commercial design and establishing her own firm in 1983. Now, Chandra finds her inspiration within the clients' personal collections, the way they live their lives, and through the home's original style, with clean lines and functional spaces defining her work.
See her work on pages 101,171,278,279
and at www.chandrastone.com

Barbara Gardner
Collins Interiors • 595 Bay Isles Road, Suite 120F, Longboat Key, FL 34228 • 941.383.0131
Whether it's a downtown condo or an expansive house on the beach, Barbara Gardner never wants a home she designed to be recognizable as one of hers. Instead, she believes each space should bring to mind its inhabitants and their personalities—never the designer. To do this, Barbara spends a lot of time getting to know her clients, from their tastes and lifestyles to even any allergies or household pets. Barbara inherited her intuitive interior design skills from several generations of family members, with particular strengths in the most effective uses of color, texture, proportion, and accessories. A student of feng shui, she had a career as a healthcare executive before founding her award-winning design firm 15 years ago.
See her work on pages 84,85,210,255
and at www.collinsinteriordesign.com

Allen Curran
Curran Cabinetry & Design • 5950 Seminole Centre Court, Suite 110, Madison, WI 53711 • 608.630.9110
Allen Curran, owner of Curran Cabinetry & Design, has been designing kitchens, baths, and furniture in the Madison area for over 37 years. He and his team often collaborate with remodeling contractors, homebuilders, and interior designers, providing custom Amish cabinetry and furniture pieces that wow homeowners and provide the type of solid construction that's dependable for decades. Allen has been certified as a kitchen designer through the National Kitchen and Bath Association, as well as a registered interior designer by the State of Wisconsin. He has won several statewide design awards with the National Kitchen and Bath Association, as well as local, regional, and national-level NARI Coty awards.
See his work on pages 140, 141, 348, 349, 371, 372, 373
and at www.currancabinetrydesign.com

Dee Frazier
Dee Frazier Interiors • 1615 Dorchester Drive, Suite 100, Plano, TX, 75075 • 972.867.2000
With a first love of graphics and project management, Dee Frazier spent over 20 years managing teams for Target department stores. In 2010, she decided to follow her dreams and opened her award-winning interior design firm. Now, she and her team revel in out-of-the-box solutions tailored to each client's home remodel. Clients love working with Dee for her unique lifestyle solutions and attention to detail when it comes to incorporating personal belongings. Solving organization and functional design dilemmas are a welcome challenge, and Dee has never met a challenge she couldn't mold into a masterpiece. Treating every project as her own, Dee and her team deliver more than expected and always within both timelines and budgets.
See her work on pages 172, 206, 246, 328
or at www.dkorhome.com

Jessica Crosby, Cate Ball, Dani Harris
Delight In Designs • 5426 Northland Drive NE, Grand Rapids, MI 49525 • 616.288.9780
From interior design to home staging to even online shopping, Delight In Designs has made it their mission to be an all-encompassing resource for the home. Led by owners Jessica Crosby and Monica Denhof, and supported by a talented team of designers, stylists, and curators, the firm expertly balances function with flair. As Jessica says, "A house is not a home until your story is attached to it," and no matter new construction or a remodel, that mantra is the guiding force for each project.
See their work on pages 154, 155, 213
and at www.delightindesigns.com

Judy Pickett
Design Lines Signature • 1611 Jones Franklin Road, Suite 103 • Raleigh, NC 27606 • 919.852.0570
Founded in 1979, Design Lines Signature is the culmination of Judy Pickett's life work—but she didn't originally set out for a career in interior design. Judy was attending Florida State University as a fashion design major when her roommate candidly shared that Judy didn't quite have the cutthroat attitude to make it in New York City's harsh world of fashion. The comment, as comical as it was, resonated with Judy and she made the choice to shift her love of textiles and art into interior design—and never looked back. Today, Judy and her team curate good design with a collaborative style in the full-service Raleigh-based firm.
See her work on pages 37, 124, 125, 228, 306-309
and at www.designlinessignature.com

Katie Ebbnes
Designers i • San Diego, CA • 505.948.2999
With a family background in custom home building and real estate, Katie Ebbens has long realized the value and importance of enjoying your surroundings. She first founded Designers i in 2010 in Albuquerque, New Mexico, but after nine years of designing for clients in the desert, she felt the beaches of Southern California calling her name. Now recognized for its warm-contemporary residential design, Designers i has projects spanning from decorating and furnishing to interior finish specification for remodeling or new construction. Katie believes that the aesthetic nature of one's space is crucial to promoting a positive and inspirational quality of living.
See her work on pages 98, 156, 157, 202
and at www.thedesignersi.com

Karen Bengel, M.Arch, ASID
Design Milieu, • Washington, D.C. • 202.297.2056
The best interior design is created, according to Karen Bengel, where art and function meet. Her comprehensive approach always addresses both, since the designer is also equipped with a master's in architecture from Virginia Tech. After graduation, she took her skills to the Washington, D.C., area in 2000, doing both commercial and residential work before opening her own firm in 2004. Now Karen focuses solely on people's homes, helping her clients discover what is unique about their tastes and lifestyle and turning that into interior spaces that beautifully serve the intimacies of life.
See her work on pages 17, 100, 170, 243, 289, 378
and at www.designmilieu.com

Diane Durocher, ASID, IIDA, CAPS, CID
Diane Durocher Interiors • Ramsey, NJ 07446 • 201.825.3832
Diane Durocher is an award-winning designer whose career spans more than 25 years. She believes that the foundation of successful design is built on trust and confidence. Connecting on a deeply personal level enables her to design inspired spaces that reflect her clients' unique personalities and lifestyles. With a keen eye for color, outstanding space-planning skills, and the ability to design customized pieces, Diane brings her clients' visions to life. She rises to the challenge of transforming a blank slate into a stunning reality. Her ultimate goal is to exceed her clients' expectations.
See her work on pages 13,54,55,196,197,238,239
and at www.dianedurocherinteriors.com

Elissa Grayer
Elissa Grayer Interior Design • 22 Purchase Street, Rye, NY 10580 • 914.921.6500
Launched in 2001, Elissa Grayer's namesake design firm quickly become the choice for young families transitioning from New York City to the idyllic suburbs of Westchester County. After graduating from Amherst College with a degree in psychology, Elissa spent 10 years in the fields of education and business, earning three masters degrees along the way. In addition, she has also studied at the prestigious New York School of Interior Design and Parsons School of Interior Design. Now, her firm has also become known for its mastery in the planning, design, and project management of grand estates, luxury apartments, and vacation retreats across New York, Connecticut, Massachusetts, and Florida.
See her work on pages 20,21,169,209,220,221,247,292,331,354,355
and at www.elissagrayerdesign.com

Esther Boivin
Esther Boivin Interiors • 7900 East Greenway Road, Suite 112, Scottsdale, AZ, 85260 • 602.549.2776
Although the connection between opera and interior design may not be immediately evident, Esther Boivin has a remarkable way of bringing these two creative forces together. Once a musician and operatic vocalist, Esther blends texture, scale, bold dynamic accents, and leitmotif to trigger desired emotional responses—just as she would with a musical composition. The result is an unmatched style that exudes transitional elegance with a bold aesthetic. Located in Scottsdale, Esther Boivin Interiors is an award-winning studio with designs completed across Arizona and all over the United States since its 2010 inception. Esther's portfolio includes residential projects from new construction, renovations, remodeling, boutique store design, restaurants, salons, and spas.
See her work on pages 9,96,242,263,270,271
and at www.estherboivininteriors.com

Aven Kaga, Design Director
GAVIN GREEN HOME DESIGN LLC – 11650 Riverside Drive, Studio City, CA 91602 – 818.351.2110
As a Parisian, Aven Kaga has lived and breathed architecture and interior design from an early age. An appetite for art has always been part of her culture, and she often gathers inspiration from her travels. Kaga's designs are about atmosphere, texture, a sense of harmony, and the comfort and pleasure of the family that lives in the home. Being based in Los Angeles means that the majority of her clients are health-conscious and tech-savvy, so her designs often incorporate the latest in technology and green wall systems for sustainability and convenience.
See her work on pages 60,61,109,150,151,194,195
www.gavingreenhomedesign.com

Ginger Atherton
Ginger Atherton & Associates • Beverly Hills, CA 90210 • 310.344.4000
Ginger Atherton designs much more than luxury interiors—she creates lifestyles. Her namesake firm began in 1986 with the idea that people want more than straightforward interior design. Ginger's A-list clients were searching for something bigger, and she delivered, making a lasting impression along the way. Known for capturing whimsy, elegance, and opulence, Ginger's spaces radiate with ultra-customized details, including personalized estate logos and luxury linens. As the pioneer of the home-staging industry in Los Angeles, Ginger knows that creating an ambience is key. Every space she designs is a celebration of something: friends, family, an event, or beautiful interiors. Private events have also become big business for Ginger, as she's taken on high-profile designs, including the green room at the Academy Awards. When Ginger's not creating sumptuous living spaces, you can find her caring for her multiple rescue dogs and miniature ponies.
See her work on pages 24,25,192,193,240,241,312,313
and at www.gingeratherton.com

Glenna Stone
Glenna Stone Interior Design • 8219 Germantown Avenue, Philadelphia, PA 19118 • 215.995.2194
Glenna Stone has discovered a successful formula for creating radiant spaces, comprised of equal parts technical skill and creative talent. Before founding Glenna Stone Interior Design in 2010, Glenna achieved a successful career in engineering. That analytical mindset in her interior design approach has proven an invaluable asset for clients. Equipped with a love of all things creative—inherited from her artist mother—Glenna designs residential and commercial spaces that capture a modern timelessness, harmony, and radiance. Inspiration comes from many sources for Glenna, but every project aims to create a sense of effortless balance, a feeling that results from a blend of style and functionality.
See her work on pages 50,51,104,130,131,297,331,360,361
and at www.glennastone.com

Sallie J. Lord
GreyHunt Interiors • Chantilly, VA 20151• 703.344.7345
Sallie J. Lord's passion for design began while working for her family's British-run furniture boutique in her teens and college years. This gave her priceless real-world experience in business and design, which she furthered with a BA in interior design from Marymount University. In 2009, she founded GreyHunt Interiors, named after her two boys, Greyson and Hunter. Sallie has gone on to proudly transform the homes and lives of countless individuals for the past 20 years. GHI transforms residential spaces by delivering accessible luxury to the Northern Virginia community and beyond. Whether full-scale or room by room, GHI always exceeds expectations by creating cohesive designs and accessible luxury. Giving back is also important to the firm, which donates time and money to causes both local and abroad.
See her work on pages 1,97,109,158,159,258,293
and at www.greyhuntinteriors.com

Karen Hattan
Home by Hattan • 5020 Marc Drive, Nashville, TN 37211• 615.202.2721
When she began her staging and design career in 2014, Karen Hattan knew she wanted to combine her passion for helping people with her passion for beautiful design. Whether a family's story includes adoption, a child with a disability or emotional need, divorce, loss, or even new beginnings, she makes sure that compassionate listening is always the first step in her process. Using a whole-family approach and a series of in-depth consultations, she then uses creative problem solving and beautiful design solutions to address any special needs and create an uplifting and supportive home for the entire family.
See her work on pages 286,287,358,359
and at www.homebyhattan.com

Jennifer Rhode
Jennifer Rhode Design • Boulder, CO 80304 • 303.362.3671
After living in Amsterdam for six years, Jennifer Rhode brought back with her the idea of "gezellig." A Dutch word meaning "coziness," the idea also encompasses social concepts like inviting or friendly. When she moved back to the States, Jennifer set out to create her own "modern gezellig" aesthetic in both her clients' homes and her own. With the belief that a modern space can be warm and inviting as well as minimal and simple, Jennifer mixes family or heritage pieces, mementos from travels, and art and photos that hold personal meaning with clean, pared-down furnishings. The result is a space that displays intriguing contrast, depth, and texture—the definition of "modern gezellig."
See her work on pages 86,87
and at www.jenniferrhode.com

Jessica Davis
JL Design • Nashville, TN 37212 • 615.321.1888
A designer's job is to push boundaries, elevate spaces, and ultimately exceed expectations. Jessica Davis of Nashville-based JL Design states that if she doesn't make a client feel a little uncomfortable, then she hasn't done her job properly. She interprets what homeowners want, even when they're not sure, and takes their style to the next level. And although she tends toward vintage modern, her designs are always a reflection of the homeowners' aesthetic, taste, and lifestyle. She works with clients to discover their passions and what they're drawn to, and provides a wide range of services to suit nearly any need. Homeowners can choose anything from new construction collaboration to custom furniture design to e-design.
See her work on pages 95,142,143,248,295, Back cover (c)
and at www.jldesignnashville.com

Kara A. Bigos
Kamarron Design Interiors, Inc. by Kara Bigos • Minneapolis, MN 55449 • 612.920.3044
Insightful, creative, and resourceful are a few designations describing the principal of this Minnesota-based firm. A master at peeking into clients' lives, Kara A. Bigos understands their wishes and is able to bring sharp spatial ingenuity to spaces. She is known for clean, classic aesthetics but always diverges to meet the uniqueness of homeowners. Kara incorporates charm to give spaces an idiosyncratic personality. Texture, color, and scale play an important role in her work. She's proven herself adept at solving challenges that may arise during projects and with varied approaches, Kara can deliver on any budget, believing that everyone should have a little luxury at home. Twenty-plus years in the industry, Kara has received many accolades including an ICFC Design Excellence Award, more than 20 National Designer of the Year Awards from IDS ,and countless others for both her residential and commercial design. Kara has served on design boards for IDS and IFDA and hosted her own radio show. She's also been a finalist multiple years for the BBB Integrity Award.
See her work on pages 11,22,23,176,205,226,227,268,269,346,347,371
and at www.kamarrondesign.com

Kathy Corbet
Kathy Corbet Interiors • 5206 Markel Road, Suite 100C, Richmond, VA 23230 • 804.310.2597
Kathy Corbet began her career in New York City's Fashion District, a creative beginning which served her well as a springboard into interior design. After moving to New England, she traded dresses for drapes and opened Kathy Corbet Interiors in 2001, and has since expanded to work with clients all over the country. Kathy and her team collaborate with top local fabricators and tradespeople to bring the clients' wishes to fruition. In fact, Kathy considers herself a chameleon of a designer and continually works to reflect the unique lifestyles and passions of each homeowner. She also gains inspiration from unexpected combinations of color, textures, patterns, and repurposed or new-found materials that she comes across during her travels.
See her work on pages 48,49,136,137,344,345,371,376
and at www.kathycorbetinteriors.com

Kimberly C. Lyons
KCL-IDESIGN, LLC • Mauldin, SC 29662 • 864.451.0068
Innately facinatedwith vibrant colors and spatial concepts, Kimberly C. Lyons felt a pull toward interior design from an early age. The innocent act of rearranging home furniture gave way to formal design studies, and eventually led Kimberly to open her South Carolina-based studio, KCL-IDESIGN, LLC, in 2011. As founder and principal designer, Kimberly finds her inspiration from several key places including international travel, striking hues, and, most importantly, God's unending creations. Nearly any pleasant aesthetic that grabs her attention can spark an idea. Kimberly's designs vary in scope and style, but she's never afraid to take risks. You'll often find urban vibes, bold artwork, and distinctive objects woven into her spaces.
See her work on pages 215,366
and at www.kcl-idesignllc.com

Kelley Proxmire
Kelley Proxmire, Inc. • 4519 Wetherill Road, Bethesda, MD 20816 • 301.320.2109
Kelley Proxmire's lifelong passion for interior design began in her parents' living room. In her pre-teen years, she was fascinated by the transformation of rooms by interior designers. "When everyone else bought *Seventeen*, I was buying *House Beautiful*, she says. Her style now is beautiful and enduring, pretty yet practical. Her projects suffuse warmth and hospitality while maintaining excellent balance, proportion, and scale. Her love of color is combined with an appreciation for the fresh sophistication of white and the daring elegance of black. Adept at mixing traditional pieces with unexpected finds, Kelley creates environments that are attuned to the client's world and faithful to the architecture and setting of a home.
See her work on pages 68,69,198,199
and at www.kelleyproxmire.com

Linda Knight Carr
Knight Carr & Company • 703 Hill Street, Greensboro, NC • 27408 • 336.370.4155
Linda Knight Carr grew up in the interior design business—quite literally. Her father owned a flooring company and when he accepted a job at the Fontainebleau Hotel in Miami, Florida, the family moved from North Carolina when Linda was just four. He soon opened his own interior design store and she played in the fabrics, sat on the worktable, and studied the accessories throughout her young years. Although it was never her intention to follow in her father's footsteps, Linda began her Greensboro-based firm Knight Carr & Company in 1985 and now works nationwide. Her only definable style is timeless beauty; Linda and her team seek to create luxury and comfort in every space.
See her work on pages 16,18,19,120,121,245,325,331,334-337,377
and at www.knightcarr.com

Kristen Pawlak, DDCD
KP Designs • 8003 Vine Crest Avenue, Suite 3, Louisville, KY 40222 • 502.245.0052
For Kristen Pawlak, design has been a lifelong love. Even as a child she would focus on rearranging furniture, the way rooms looked, and finding different perspectives. Kristen found herself in a marketing consultant career as an adult and later realized that her childhood passion should be her full-time pursuit. Kristen opened KP Designs in 2009, where she and her team interpret client's wishes into classic styles with modern touches. With a careful attention to detail, Kristen and her team work out a comprehensive plan before beginning a project to ensure its success. Her work reflects the lifestyle and preferences of the homeowner, blended with her inspirations from travel, art, history, and natural surroundings.
See her work on pages 17,107,296,326,368
and at www.kpdesigns.decoratingden.com

Laurie McRae
Laurie McRae Interiors • 1325 Troupe Street • Augusta, GA 30904 • 706.863.5440
Laurie McRae owns and operates her full-service namesake firm, offering residential and commercial clients more than 35 years of interior design experience. Aiming for timelessness, Laurie's designs eschew passing fads to focus on personalized form and function that is as beautiful as it is smart. In addition to holding a board-member position with the Georgia State Licensing Board of Architects and Interior Designers, Laurie is certified by the National Council of Interior Design Qualification and has served on that international board as president. She also has the Associate Kitchen and Bath Designer certification from the National Kitchen and Bath Association, and is a fine art appraiser. She lends her time to causes dear to her, including work with Hope House for women and Historic Augusta annual antique benefits.
See her work on pages 7,40,41,108, 100,111,249,280,281,327
and at www.lauriemcrae.com

Lucy Emory Hendricks
Legacy Interiors • 4016 Highway 17 S, North Myrtle Beach, SC 29582 • 843.427.4159
A straight shooter with a large dose of Southern charm, Lucy Emory Hendricks is never afraid to roll up her sleeves and get the job done. She began as a buyer for one of the country's largest outdoor furniture companies before transitioning to a full-service design firm, and then opening her own company over a decade ago. This all totals more than 25 years in the industry, and through it all she has learned that the more she understands her clients and their lifestyles, the better equipped she is to transform their environments into beautiful spaces to live in and celebrate both the big and small moments in life.
See her work on pages 11,106,160,161,298,350,351
and at www.legacyinteriorssc.com

Linda G. Burnside
LGB Interiors • 614 Hilton Street • Columbia, SC 29205 • 803.929.5322
Linda Burnside has an arsenal of coveted design awards under her belt, along with national and international recognition in a variety of publications. Her down-to-earth personality makes this all the more impressive, and she goes into every project with a focus on the client's lifestyle. Since beginning her namesake firm, LGB Interiors, in 1987, Linda has worked on nearly every type of project imaginable–from ground-up home design, to small-space renovations. Her time spent designing for luxury resorts and boutique hotels shows up in her residential work, as each project has the distinct feel of a destination.
See her work on pages 10.42,43,126,127,179,188,189,232,233,307,324,363
and at www.lgbinteriors.com

Lisa Gielincki
Lisa Gielincki Interior Design • 13500 Sutton Park Drive South, Suite 101, Jacksonville, FL 32224 • 904.821.8891
No two projects are alike, and Lisa Gielincki prefers it that way. She and her team work collaboratively on each project, bringing multiple perspectives into balance and ensuring a deeply considered result. For each one, it's critical that she understands the client's vision thoroughly. She then draws upon her aesthetic ability, project management experience, and strong relationships with builders, craftspeople, artisans, and other talented partners to execute the vision seamlessly. Every detail that matters to her clients matters even more to Lisa and her team. As she has learned throughout her career, good interior design often looks effortless, but behind the scenes a great deal of effort is poured into every detail.
See her work on pages 44,45,132,133,263,272,273,342,343,Back cover(L)
and at www.lisaginteriordesign.com

Lori Carroll
Lori Carroll & Associates • 2496 East River Road, Suite 100, Tucson, AZ 85718 • 520.886.3443
Specializing in luxury residential spaces, Lori Carroll creates singular, eclectic spaces that push the envelope of interior design. Never afraid to take a risk, Lori Carroll and her team utilize a wide variety of materials, colors, and textures–sometimes in the most unexpected ways–to catch your eye. The manner in which she incorporates these elements into a space is what makes her firm stand out. Based in Tucson, Arizona, Lori Carroll has worked all over the Southwest, including California and northern Mexico as well as Chicago and New York. She uses the natural environment, in combination with the homeowner's lifestyle, to inspire her designs.
See her work on pages 26,27,116,117,262,264-267,307,310,311,375
and at www.loricarroll.com

Lori Graham
Lori Graham Design + HOME • Washington, DC • 202.745.0118
Lori Graham, founder of Lori Graham Design–a Washington, D.C.-based design firm with clients nationwide–is known for her use of fresh colors, layers of texture, and mix of modern materials. Lori's clients have described her designs as "comfortably chic" and as "curated comfort." Although Lori has lived around the world, she has called Washington, D.C. home where she's owned and operated her firm since 2003, and the online lifestyle showroom since 2012. Formerly an attorney, Lori's path to a design career was anything but traditional. Before leaving the practice of law, Lori renovated three personal residences, experiencing the homeowner's point of view firsthand. Lori credits these experiences, along with her first career, for the fundamentals of her design business: precision, professionalism, and perspective.
See her work on pages 32,33,184,185,224,225,352,353
and at www.lorigraham.com

Melanie King
Melanie King Designs • Houston and The Woodlands, TX • 832.647.9203
With degrees in both interior design and international studies, Melanie King has traveled the world exploring diverse cultures and architectural movements, bringing all that she's learned back to her nationally acclaimed design firm. Melanie understands that design is a living process, and delivers dynamic ideas within a thoughtful, detail-oriented approach before guiding her clients through each step of the installation. She's able to take any vision and transform it into a tangible space where you can live, rest, and entertain. Above all, she believes that great design happens when a passion for beauty is united with exceptional craftsmanship and superior attention to detail.
See her work on pages 94,167,256,263,299
and at www.melaniekingdesigns.com

Michelle Lynne
ML Interiors Group • Dallas, TX • 972.248.4733
Michelle Lynne's interior design story begins where her corporate life ended. After some major changes in her big-business management job, Michelle found herself praying and asking "What's next?" Her answer came in the form of her lifelong passion: interior design. In 2008, Michelle started ML Interiors Group as a one-woman show and has since expanded the operation to include a team of talented women. Continually collaborating, the crew takes a smart, stylish, and fun approach to every project. Michelle has shared her firm's methods by developing a new division of her brand called Designed for the Creative Mind®. This is a platform she created for all interior designers to learn the ins and outs of running a successful interior design business.
See her work on pages 8,28,29,118,119,180,181,222,223,356,357,369,374,Back cover (R)
and at www.mlinteriorsgroup.com

Molly Gilbertson
M Gilbertson Design • 6581 Cherokee Trail West, Eden Prairie, MN 55344 • 952.906.9628
With more than 20 years of design experience, owner and principal designer Molly Gilbertson has built her award-winning firm into a resource that clients turn to again and again for design expertise, genuine friendship, and her sense of style. She's proud to not be a "one and done" type of designer, but instead forms relationships that last through several years—and projects. Aided by her longtime design assistant Leah Kirkhorn, Molly creates spaces that range from modern to traditional to everything in between, always reflecting the clients' dreams and aspirations while remaining firmly within budget.
See her work on pages 90,91,173,362
and at www.mgilbertsondesign.com

Pamela O'Brien
Pamela Hope Designs • Houston, TX • 713.880.1934
An award-winning luxury interior designer, writer, and speaker, Pamela O'Brien has been celebrated for mastering the art and science of designing custom spaces that make people feel at home. A lifelong passion for art and culture and living abroad led her to attending a professional development program at the Harvard Graduate School of Design. Twenty years later Pamela is a respected figure in Houston design and philanthropy circles. A frequent traveler and curious by nature, Pamela crosses the globe regularly, speaks fluent French and Italian, and enjoys educating audiences through the National Speakers Association and the American Society of Interior Designers.
See her work on pages 12,92,168,179,208,300
and at www.pamelahopedesigns.com

Patrice Rios
Patrice Rios Interiors • 4646 Meuller Blvd • Austin, TX 78723 • 512.810.3730
After receiving a masters of architecture from the University of Detroit Mercy, Patrice Rios began her career at age 21. She started by accepting a senior position designing luxury hotels in Shanghai, then moved to Austin, where she later founded her first company, Troo Design, at the age of 28. Patrice has been featured on HGTV's *Container Homes*, after taking shipping containers and converting them into livable, modern homes. She's also been a reoccurring design consultant on *Buying & Selling* with the Property Brothers. Patrice is currently lead designer for The Colton House, an 80-room boutique hotel located on South Congress in Austin, Texas.
See her work on pages 165, 282,283,364
or at www.patricerios.com

Sheeja Nair
Raashi Design • San Ramon, CA 94582 • 925.236.0402
Sheeja Nair has been interested in art and design since childhood, but while building her own custom home she realized her passion and talent for interior design. Sheeja eventually decided to pursue interior design full-time, founding Raashi Design in 2012. Today, the award-winning interior design and decorating firm is known for its unique, inspiring designs and exceptional customer focus, serving the San Francisco Bay area as well as India. Working in different parts of the world has influenced Sheeja's design style and perspective in a truly global way. She has a unique approach to colors, textures, space organization, and lighting, and prides herself on out-of-the-box solutions to challenging design problems. In addition to interior design training, Sheeja has master's degrees in physics and computer engineering.
See her work on pages 70,71,144,145
and at www.raashidesign.com

James Rill
Rill Architects • 4833 Rugby Avenue, Bethesda, MD 20814 • 301.656.4166
From small-scale renovations to large, single-family homes, Rill Architects has been designing custom residences, renovations, and additions since 1987. The firm is equally at home designing traditional and modern projects, working closely with clients to create spaces that are both innovative and tasteful, and that respond to homeowners' unique personalities, lifestyles, and needs. Founder and principal James Rill cultivates team spirit among his colleagues by ensuring that they remain involved in every phase of the project. James and his team carefully consider clients' goals while guiding them through the complexities of the design and other processes. This sense of collaboration exists not only within Rill Architects, but also extends between the firm, its clients, and the contractors.
See his work on pages 14,72,73,316,317
and at www.rillarchitects.com

Shakirah Fayson
Sanctuary Rooms • Glenarden, MD • 301.655.9137
Washington, D.C.-area native Shakirah Fayson is gifted with an innate affection for all things artistic. Whether it's the performing arts—her former life was as a classically trained dancer—or interior architecture and design, she brings a keen eye and fierce work ethic to every project she's involved in. Shakirah comes from a long line of businesswomen, entrepreneurs, and creatives, and that's inevitably what spurred her to attend the master's I.A.D program at the Academy of Art in Los Angeles and then train under some of the most seasoned designers in the country. The unabridged passion to create design solutions, find unique furniture pieces, and transform spaces that capture the individuality and personality of each client is what sets her firm, Sanctuary Rooms, apart.
See her work on pages 78,79,367,380
and at www.sanctuaryrmz.net

Tanya Shively
Sesshu Design Associates • 3666 N Miller Rd, Suite 100, Scottsdale, AZ 85251 • 480.436.7766
Raised next to the Grand Tetons in Wyoming, designer Tanya Shively grew up with a love and appreciation for hard work, nature, and environmental stewardship. She founded Sesshu Design Associates in 2005 with the belief that healthy and sustainable homes should be the standard, and has since built her reputation as a designer by creating healthy homes in Scottsdale, Arizona, by using materials that are free of the toxins that can bring on health issues for the inhabitants. But she never compromises on quality or finishes, dedicating her career to designing interiors that become a sanctuary for resting, relaxing, and enjoying life.
See her work on pages 80,81,338,339
and at www.sesshudesign.com

Shannon Antipov
Shannon Antipov Designs • 5762 South Garfield Street, Hinsdale, IL, 60521 • 574.485.9528
Often, Shannon Antipov can walk into a home and immediately spot its potential, seeing possibilities that no one else can. And once you imagine it, she often says, you can make it a reality. She constantly moved around early in her adult life, and since she couldn't design her dream home for so long, she channeled her passion and skills into doing it for others. Making people's lives happier through design is what drives her, and Shannon never gets tired of seeing her clients' eyes light up when they see the magic she's accomplished.
See her work on pages 17,82,83,200,201
and at www.shannonantipovdesigns.com

Elizabeth O'Neal
Southern Studio • 119 West Park Street, Cary, NC 27511 • 919.362.5143
Elizabeth has always been intrigued by the way people live in their homes, and an interior design class in high school was the first stepping stone toward turning her dream into a career. After attending an accredited design college, she jumped right into the industry. With a personal style she describes as sophisticated transitional, Elizabeth focuses on functional rooms with a soft color palette, luxurious textures, clean lines, and unexpected accessories and finishes.
See her work on pages 34,35,122,123,260,329,340,341
and at www.southernstudio.com

Vicky Serany
Southern Studio • 119 West Park Street, Cary, NC 27511 • 919.362.5143
As head of the collaborative design team, Vicky encourages each member to bring a fresh perspective to a project while also encouraging clients' participation. She delights in working on vacation homes, which often end up being some of her favorite projects. Vicky uses fresh combinations of texture, pattern, and color, paying attention to every detail of a project to meticulously transform the vision into reality. Her inspiration comes from the beauty in everyday life and travel to fascinating places.
See her work on pages 34,35,122,123,260,329,340,341
and at www.southernstudio.com

Shane Spencer
Spencer Design Associates • Minneapolis, MN • 612.440.2255
A lover of color, emerging art and sculpture, and incredible light fixtures, Shane Spencer brings sophistication and an eclectic yet casual feel to every environment his studio creates. The philosophy is simple: Create meaningful spaces that are a true reflection of the unique style and vision of each client. By utilizing a wide range of architectural and design styles, his studio develops rooms that are balanced, refined, curated, and layered, forging elements together that imbue these environments with a sense of intrigue and curiosity. Shane believes in design as storytelling and the Studio prides itself on developing an individual identity and graphic dialogue for each of their projects while delivering a result that is better than their clients could have imagined.
See his work on pages 8,74,75,93,128,129,301
and at www.spencerdesignassociates.com

Elizabeth Scruggs
Superior Construction and Design • Lebanon, TN 37087 • 615.969.3354
Walking into a room produces either a good or a bad feeling, and Elizabeth Scruggs has made it her mission to create as many good feelings as possible. With more than 20 years of experience in construction, interior and exterior design, and color specification, she and her team help homeowners narrow down the seemingly endless options into a beautiful home that perfectly suits their needs and wants. From the initial design inception to constructing the completed project—everything from flooring and furnishings to accessories and even grout color—Elizabeth handles it all, focusing on the end feeling that makes it all worth it.
See her work on pages 175,303
and at www.scdtn.com

Susan Semmelmann
Susan Semmelmann Interiors • 4372 West Vickery Boulevard Fort Worth, TX 76107 • 940.577.1000
Each design from Susan Semmelmann Interiors is as singular as the client, with its own character, beauty, and intricacies. The namesake firm is owned and operated by Susan herself, who has worked in the world of building and design for more than two decades. A giver at heart, she founded the Dallas-Fort Worth-based company on the idea that spaces within a home are personal, and they have the unique ability to influence experiences and memories. When properly designed, interiors can enhance everyday life, and as Susan says, "Home is our happy place, it's where we find life." Outside of the firm, Susan remains involved in the community and works with charities that are dear to her.
See her work on pages 30,31,166,204, 216,218,219,284,285,Back flap
and at www.semmelmanninteriors.com

Tanga Winstead
Tanga Winstead Designs • 4882 Annunciation Street, New Orleans, LA 70115 • 504.329.1929
Looking back, Tanga Winstead has been drawn to design ever since she can remember. What seemed like hobbies—rearranging furniture, painting walls, accessorizing her room—were actually the early signs of a lifelong passion. Tanga eventually found her way into interior design through fashion and the retail industry, which helped develop her love of color, texture, and form. She has studied and traveled extensively but found her home in New Orleans, where she has established her namesake firm, Tanga Winstead Designs, and carved out her niche. Artistic, eclectic, and full of life, the spaces that Tanga designs are reflections of the homeowners' desires and an homage to her endless creativity and enthusiasm for interiors and problem-solving.
See her work on pages 62,63,211,257,302,381
and at www.tangawinstead.com

Nancy Black, Brent Willmott, Kat Black
Total 360 Interiors, Inc. • 2323 N. Houston Street, Suite 511, Dallas, TX 75219 • 214.226.2034 / 214.534.2342
In 2002, Nancy Black and Brent Willmott made the life-changing decision to jump headfirst into their favorite hobby: designing spaces. Working corporate jobs and flipping houses on the side, they were both burnt out on their full-time jobs. They craved creativity so much that they opened Total 360 Interiors and invested themselves completely in the Dallas-based firm. Six years later, Kat Black joined the team and has brought her passion for well-planned spaces to the table. The trio prides themselves on elegant, contemporary design and thoughtfully curated rooms. They offer commercial and residential design, space planning, concept development, remodeling, custom furnishings, interior restyling, and color consultation.
See their work on pages 46,47,134,135,217,234,235,304,370,379
and at www.total360interiors.com

Lauren and Wendy Nolan-Sellers
Trust the Vision Decor • Philadelphia, PA • 267.438.5318
"Create. Innovate. Decorate." That's the motto of Trust the Vision Decor, which Lauren and Wendy Nolan-Sellers founded in 2012. After excelling as a teacher, Lauren underwent a life-changing experience with their difficult first pregnancy and switched to her true passion, interior design. Now, Trust the Vision Decor has become her successful second act, with the couple helping Philadelphians turn their homes into stylish havens—always on time and under budget. This two-women team has been named to the Best of Houzz List every year since 2015 and has celebrated these distinctions in both design and customer service. Most recently, the pair has enjoyed features in both *Architectural Digest* and on the NBC *Today Show*. They continue to thrive, cultivating relationships and transforming lives through their gift of interior design.
See their work on pages 174,253
and at www.trustthevisiondecor.com

Jessica Love, Allied ASID
Urbane Design • 4107 Medical Parkway, Suite 212, Austin, TX 78756 • 512.522.6035
Jessica Love learned the rules of the interior design trade early so that she can now—strategically—break them. A graduate of Sam Houston State University with a bachelor of science in interior design, Jessica believes in individuality over trends and works to bring her clients' personalities through in each design. Whenever possible, she and her team breathe new life into antique furniture, art, and accessories, and new materials are selected with longevity in mind. A long-time volunteer with several nonprofit organizations around Austin, Jessica also has her own nonprofit, Design Changes Lives, which helps design spaces for children in order to build confidence and improve the quality of their lives.
See her work on pages 274,275
and at www.urbanedesignstudios.com

www.ingramcontent.com/pod-product-compliance
Lightning Source LLC
Chambersburg PA
CBHW051309110526
44590CB00031B/4351